NEW DIRECTIONS IN SCANDINAVIAN STUDIES

Terje Leiren and Christine Ingebritsen, Series Editors

NEW DIRECTIONS IN SCANDINAVIAN STUDIES

This series offers interdisciplinary approaches to the study of the Nordic region of Scandinavia and the Baltic States and their cultural connections in North America. By redefining the boundaries of Scandinavian studies to include the Baltic States and Scandinavian America, the series presents books that focus on the study of the culture, history, literature, and politics of the North.

Small States in International Relations
edited by Christine Ingebritsen, Iver B. Neumann,
Sieglinde Gstöhl, and Jessica Beyer

Danish Cookbooks: Domesticity and National Identity, 1616–1901 by Carol Gold

Crime and Fantasy in Scandinavia: Fiction, Film, and Social Change by Andrew Nestingen

Selected Plays of Marcus Thrane by Terje I. Leiren

Munch's Ibsen: A Painter's Visions of a Playwright
by Joan Templeton

Selected Plays of MARCUS THRANE

Translated with Introduction by

Terje I. Leiren

The Norwegian-American Historical Association
Northfield, Minnesota
IN ASSOCIATION WITH
University of Washington Press • Seattle, Washington

The Norwegian-American Historical Association (NAHA) was organized on 6 October 1925 by a group of far-sighted Norwegian Americans who sought to establish a national center for the collection and preservation of historical material. Theirs was a practical as well as a thoroughly professional endeavor to provide funds for the publication of interesting books by talented scholars, who by careful research and interpretation would describe the American experience of an immigrant people then firmly rooted in the new world. The association has enjoyed success and gained the recognition and respect of an international scholarly community. In fulfillment of its purpose, the association has published more than ninety books of scholarly merit, promoted Norwegian-American historical research and literary work, and helped maintain and develop archives at St. Olaf College of Norwegian-American historical material. This rich program has attracted to the association a membership of 2,000 citizens from all walks of life.

This publication is supported by a grant from the Scandinavian Studies Publication Fund.

Printed in the United States of America

Norwegian-American Historical Association
1510 St. Olaf Avenue
Northfield, MN 55057-1097, USA
www.naha.stolaf.edu

University of Washington Press
PO Box 50096
Seattle, WA 98145-5096, USA
www.washington.edu/uwpress

ISBN 978-0-295-98798-9

The paper used in this publication meets the minimum requirements of American National Standard for Information Sciences-Permanence of Paper for Printed Library Materials, ANSI Z39.48-1984.

to AnnaTheresa, Kari Marie,
Hunter Eilif, and Markus Kristian

CONTENTS

Marcus Thrane

FOREWORD

Perhaps as much as any other figure, Marcus Thrane (1817–1890) represents the transatlantic character of life in Norway and the United States during the period of the great migration. In both nations he embodied the spirit of European nineteenth-century revolutionary movements. As a young man in Norway, Thrane organized labor societies that included both urban and rural members. His agitation resulted in the presentation of a petition for redress of grievances to the king signed by thousands, and proposals for reform brought to the attention the Norwegian parliament. This proved too much for the authorities, who saw to the arrest of Thrane and more than a hundred other labor leaders. Tried and found guilty for opinion rather than action, Thrane was sentenced to four years in prison. On his release he found the movement he had organized in disarray, and he himself departed for the United States.

Thrane took his causes with him to America and quickly emerged as a critic of the government, the economic order, social structures, and what he perceived to be the narrowness of Norwegian-American life. As a writer, speaker, and editor, he showed himself a keen observer and critic of both the larger American society and the smaller ethnic community to which he belonged. He wrote and spoke with a sensibility sharpened by a capacity to compare the situation in the United States with that in Europe.

Among a number of more and less successful ventures in the United States, Thrane wrote and produced a number of plays for Norwegian-speaking audiences in America. The plays are of modest literary quality, but as entertainment and dramatically presented argument they tell us much about the author and his audiences. They continue to invite reading and may yet evoke a smile, agreement, or an argument from contemporary readers. They may do all three.

The Norwegian-American Historical Association is indebted to Professor Terje I. Leiren for selecting the plays included in the present volume, for his able translations, and for introductory comments and notes.

Sylvia Ruud designed the book, created the dustjacket, and guided production. I am again grateful on behalf of all of our readers to the board of directors of the Norwegian-American Historical Association for its unflagging support of the organization's publications.

Todd W. Nichol
Editor

PREFACE

This book presents a selection of plays by Marcus Thrane translated from the original Norwegian-language manuscripts located in the National Library in Oslo, Norway. The manuscripts, along with personal notes and memoirs, were deposited in the National Library by Thrane's American descendants, who had kept the material after his death on April 30, 1890.

Marcus Thrane wrote more than twenty plays. Some of these are known to have been lost and some were only partially completed. The six plays included here are especially representative of Thrane's authorship and give a comprehensive picture of his cultural and political views that may also have reflected the views of a large number of other immigrants to the United States in the nineteenth century. The plays are arranged chronologically and cover the entire period of his active political and cultural engagement in America from 1866 to 1884. *An American Servant Girl* was written and produced in Thrane's first years in Chicago and represents an overwhelmingly optimistic view of the immigrant experience. *Holden* and *The Power of the Black Book* were written and produced in the first half of the 1880s, after Thrane had developed a more skeptical view of both America and the immigration process and was himself approaching the end of his professional career.

The Posting Station in Hallingdal was probably Thrane's favorite play. Written for the Norwegian Theater in Chicago, it was performed four times in 1867–1868. Thrane called it a "national musical," probably because it contained echoes of popular presentations from the Norwegian National Romantic period of his youth. *The Hypocrites* and *Who Grinds the Coffee* may be Thrane's most timeless plays. Both deal with issues that remain relevant in the twenty-first century, religious hypocrisy and questions of gender equality. In each of the plays in this collection, America plays a symbolic role, subtle yet significant, almost as one of the characters. The plays were, after all, written primarily for a

Norwegian-American audience experiencing and adapting to immigrant life in America and all the complexities that were involved in that process.

I greatly appreciate the support I have received in the process of working with Thrane's plays. During the several occasions when I presented papers discussing one or more of Thrane's plays, I received important feedback from colleagues. These comments often helped me better to understand the plays and the immigrant culture out of which they grew and to which they appealed. I especially want to thank Odd Lovoll, the former editor of the Norwegian-American Historical Association, for his encouragement, friendship, and support in the beginning of this project. Discussions with friends, colleagues, and respected scholars including Orm Øverland, Ingeborg Kongslien, Dag Blanck, Byron Nordstrom, Lee Sather, Helge Pharo, and the late Ingrid Semmingsen, were of immense help to me and are greatly appreciated. I also want to thank Todd Nichol, present NAHA editor, for his support and work in shepherding this manuscript to publication. Likewise, I want to acknowledge the work of the editorial staff at the University of Washington Press, especially Executive Editor Michael Duckworth. An important contribution to the sparse material relating to Marcus Thrane is a six-volume typescript of Thrane's plays made by Jorun Marie Jonassen of Trondheim in 1984 in connection with a radio production about Marcus Thrane on Norway's Radio P-2. Those programs, based to a large extent on the original manuscript of my 1987 book, *Marcus Thrane: An American Radical in America*, published by the Norwegian-American Historical Association, were produced by Arild Hoksnes and Jan Ragnar Hagland and broadcast several times in Norway.

A research stay at the History Department at the University of Bergen as part of the University of Washington/University of Bergen faculty exchange program gave me the opportunity to complete both research details and the final translations of the manuscripts. Members of the staff at the *Håndskriftsavdeling* of the National Library in Oslo, especially Sigbjørn Grindheim, were particularly helpful, as was Einar Thomassen of the manuscript and newspaper section at the University of Bergen Library. Travel support on two occasions from the Norwegian Ministry of Foreign Affairs through the Norwegian Information Service in New York aided my work on this project considerably. The University of Washington, through my home Department of Scandinavian Studies and the Office of the Dean of Arts and Sciences, deserves special thanks for their approval of sabbatical leave that allowed me to complete the project. I also want to express my sincere appreciation to Espen Børhaug, in Bergen, for his most generous gesture of providing access to his apartment during an extended stay there. Finally, to Ingunn, a special thanks for her support, but mostly her love. This book is dedicated to four members of our family's youngest generation. May they always treasure their Norwegian heritage.

Terje I. Leiren
Seattle, Washington

INTRODUCTION: MARCUS THRANE AND THE NORWEGIAN THEATER IN AMERICA

ETHNIC THEATER IN THE UNITED STATES traces its traditions back to the rituals and communal celebrations of Native Americans and the European slave ships that brought Africans to the shores of the western hemisphere. Well-established French theater came to the United States with the transfer of the Louisiana Territory in 1803, and Spanish-language theater followed soon after with the transfer of Florida in 1819 and the conquest of the Southwest in the 1840s. European theater also arrived in the nineteenth century. The German theater dates from around 1840, Norwegian and Swedish theater from the 1860s, Yiddish theater from the 1880s, and Polish theater from the decade of the 1890s. Chinese theater traces its life in America from the 1890s.[1]

One of the early ethnic theaters in America was the Norwegian Theater of Marcus Thrane, established in Chicago in September 1866. For the next eighteen months Thrane wrote, directed, and produced his own plays, while he also presented plays from Scandinavia, including several from the Danish theatrical tradition as well as material from the National Romantic period in Norway. He frequently also wrote or adapted the music that accompanied the plays, his own as well as those of other authors. The original plays of Marcus Thrane were probably among the most significant Norwegian-American literary works produced in America at this time. His plays not only represented the author's own vision, but also echoed the voices of Norwegian immigrants in their desire to accommodate themselves to their new home while remembering the land they left behind. Because their memories of Norway were both good and bad, it often meant that there were occasional, and sometimes far from subtle, political references in Thrane's plays. These references could be to the economic difficulties or they could be comments on the class inequality

[1]Maxine Schwartz Seller, "Introduction," in *Ethnic Theatre in the United States*, edited by Maxine Schwartz Seller (Westport, Connecticut, 1983), 3–17.

that existed in Norway. Whatever the subtext might be, the audiences understood and probably often shared the views expressed on the stage. Thrane's Norwegian Theater and the plays it presented, whether set in America or in Norway, can be seen as a deliberate attempt by Thrane to establish a Norwegian-American cultural alternative in line with his political views and in opposition to the overwhelming cultural dominance of the Norwegian-American clergy. For Marcus Thrane, this meant presenting plays that focused on the conflicts between the Norwegian-American clergy and Freethinkers, between science and superstition, and between the old world and the new, often while emphasizing the benefits of American liberty and personal freedom.

Although they had softer edges, Thrane's plays were not dissimilar to his political writings and speeches. In his speeches and published essays, Thrane could frequently rail against the clergy as anachronistic and irrelevant in nineteenth-century society. He distrusted the state as an active agent for moral change or social legislation, believing these matters to be the responsibility of the independent citizenry. He wrote frequently against the collective concepts of many contemporary socialists, arguing instead for a respect for private property and the fruits of hard work. In addition, he had a generally optimistic faith in the idea of progress and the benefits of education and enlightenment. Thrane's and the Norwegian Theater's play-evenings thus served several didactic functions. In addition to being general entertainment and occasions for social get-togethers for an immigrant community, they were also the forceful expressions of a radical political leader, labor organizer, and social critic.[2] This is not surprising in view of his earlier career in Norway. There he had been a teacher who, in the wake of the political unrest and revolutionary spirit abounding in 1848, worked briefly as a newspaper editor before emerging as a labor leader and organizer.

Marcus Thrane was born in Norway on 14 October 1817, into a wealthy merchant family in Christiania (Oslo). He was the youngest of

[2]Thrane's political views were expressed most profoundly in *Dagslyset*, a monthly newspaper that he published between 1869 and 1878. Numerous articles written by Thrane during this time reflect ideas similar to those broached in his plays. See, for example, "Mormonerne," in *Dagslyset*, June 1870, where Thrane defends the Mormon church's right to polygamy based on his belief that it is an expression of religious liberty under the American Constitution. See, also, "Forholdet imellem Socialisme og Fritænkning," *Dagslyset*, April 1877, and for his opposition to collective ownership, see Thrane's report on his visit to socialist and freethinker communities in Kansas in "Fra mine Reiser," *Dagslyset*, January, February, and July, 1872. One can also see Thrane's first public acknowledgment of his anticlerical views in "Det norske Præsteværldet i Amerika," in *Marcus Thrane's Norske Amerikaner*, 29 July 1866.

three surviving children. His sister, Camilla, was four years his senior, and his brother, David, three years older. His grandfather, Paul Thrane, had built a successful business in grain and timber sales and was one of the city's prominent citizens. In the same year of the birth of Marcus, Paul Thrane was elected to the Norwegian parliament but, due to illness, he was not able to attend the short three-month triennial session in early 1818.

Marcus Thrane grew up in a family interested in theater and surrounded by music. His uncle, Waldemar Thrane, gained prominence as a violinist and as the composer of one of Norway's earliest folk operas, *Fjeldeventyret* [*Mountain Adventure*]. His father, David, was a member of an Oslo dramatic society when, in 1802, he married another member, Helene Sophie Bull, daughter of a wealthy Fredrikstad merchant. Helene appears to have been a rebellious child who distressed her parents in 1794 when she left a would-be groom standing at the altar. It is safe to conclude that Marcus Thrane grew up significantly influenced by the interests and personalities of both his parents.[3]

Economic bad luck and poor decisions led Thrane's father into troubled financial waters. Arrested for using bank funds to finance private investments, David Thrane was judged guilty of misappropriating funds in 1820. Paul Thrane and friends helped David avoid prison by raising 99,513 *speciedaler* to repay the funds. However, as a result, the family was financially devastated. Only two months old when the storm broke in 1817, Marcus grew up in déclassé poverty, drawn to *belles lettres*, the classics, romances, tragedies, and comedies. History, he later wrote, did not interest him.[4]

At the age of twenty-one in the summer of 1838, Thrane took his savings of thirty *riksdaler* and went on a romantic adventure to the European continent. Traveling initially through the Rhineland and Switzerland, he arrived in Paris with his money spent. Arrested for vagrancy, he was eventually released and returned to Norway through the assistance of the Swedish-Norwegian consul. In the meantime, the vagabond student had observed French culture and probably also encountered some of the revolutionary ideas that like an unseen virus floated in the Parisian air at the time. Back in Norway, he enrolled at the university, where he studied theology. In his reminiscences, Thrane later wrote that he was already ques-

[3]Halvdan Koht, *Marcus Thrane, til hundreaarsdagen, 14 oktober* (Kristiania, 1917), 5–6. See also Oddvar Bjørklund, *Marcus Thrane: sosialistleder i et u-land* (Oslo, 1970).

[4]Marcus Thrane, "Autobiographical Reminiscences," translated by Vasilia Thrane Struck, in Marcus Thrane Papers, National Library, Oslo.

tioning social norms and established religion, perhaps ideas he brought back with him from the continent.[5]

In August, 1841, he married Josephine Buch, with whom he established a private school in Lillehammer. As a teacher, Thrane used drama and theater as a part of his instruction. It appears he also wrote for and acted in amateur theater groups during the five years he was in Lillehammer. In addition, he organized a group of musicians to complement the theatrical performances. The repertoire, mostly traditional, included works by authors such as Ludvig Holberg, Erik Bøgh, and Adam Oehlenschläger, among others. Thrane also wrote some of the material the groups performed.[6]

In 1846, Thrane moved his school, and his family, to Åsgårdstrand near Tønsberg. After a year he took a teaching position at the Modum Cobalt Works [*Blåfarveverket*], teaching the children of the workers there. In 1848, the revolutions on the continent caught up with the restless young teacher. One day he picked up the Oslo newspaper *Morgenbladet* and his life took a decisive turn. The laboring classes of Europe were demanding a voice in government, he wrote, and "herewith came light to my gropings! I believed that my dreams might perhaps be realized."[7]

Thrane left the school and, in August 1848, became editor of *Drammens Adresse*, a small regional paper in Drammen, a port city southeast of Modum. As editor, he echoed many of the themes from the uprising on the continent when he criticized what he perceived to be the injustices in Norwegian society, especially the lack of political and liberal democracy. He wrote in support of guaranteed wages for workers and loans to purchase inexpensive housing, while criticizing the practice of the rich of escaping military service by paying a fee. His provocative comments frightened many and, when subscriptions declined, Thrane was dismissed after only four months as editor. Undeterred, however, he continued to work to further his ideas by beginning the first effort to organize the Norwegian lower classes "in accordance with French ideas."[8]

On December 27, Marcus Thrane established the first labor association, with 160 members. By the following spring, ten associations had been formed and on May 5, the premier issue of *Arbeiderforeningernes*

[5]Thrane, "Autobiographical Reminiscences," Marcus Thrane Papers.

[6]G. F. Gunnersen, *Lillehammer i Nitti Aar, 1827–1917* (Lillehammer, 1917), 304; Oddvar Bjørklund, *Marcus Thrane*, 29–30.

[7]Thrane, "Autobiographical Reminiscences," in Marcus Thrane Papers.

[8]Thrane, "Autobiographical Reminiscences, " Marcus Thrane Papers.

Blad [*The Labor Associations' Newspaper*] appeared. Through the newspaper and in public speeches, complemented by a remarkable organizational talent, Thrane spread the word for worker unity and political reform. At its height, the movement may have had as many as 30,000 members. Thrane's rhetoric was always crisp and his writings poignant and strident as he attacked the establishment of both church and state.

The political program articulated by Thrane called for radical social and political reform in Norway if not a socialist revolution. He traveled extensively, lecturing and spreading a new gospel of worker unity. *Arbeiderforeningernes Blad* carried articles attacking the privileges of wealth and the miserable conditions of the urban and rural poor, especially the landless cotter class [*husmenn*]. Thrane's agitation signaled a rising popular movement for reform and the emergence of a class movement in Norway.

In the spring of 1850, probably inspired by the English Chartist movement, Thrane and his friend Paul Hjelm-Hansen, a lawyer, wrote a petition to the king listing ten grievances that the associations sought to redress. The petition, including 12,833 signatures, expressed loyalty to the monarch at the same time as it sought substantial political and economic reform. The demands included a call for the abolition of limitations on free trade and the elimination of harmful tariffs on imported necessities. Likewise, the petition urged the improvement of the condition of the cotters by allowing them to purchase their own land. In addition to demanding universal suffrage, the petition also called for universal military service, reforms in the judicial system, and better schools. While the petition ultimately fell on deaf ears, Thrane maintained an optimistic view that he would eventually change society by helping to enlighten his fellow Norwegians. Most significant, in this regard, was the importance of a cultural component for the labor movement, especially the use of song and theater to inform, brighten, and entertain. Thrane clearly recognized the importance of music and song in developing feelings of solidarity, a significant anticipation of the role of music in the international labor movement as it developed in the following century.

A lengthy article by Thrane in *Arbeiderforeningernes Blad*, in March 1850, discussed the essential nature of a popular theater that would offer plays for enlightenment as well as entertainment. Thrane believed that free time and the enjoyment of art were essential in order for workers to escape labor's oppressive conditions and life's trivialities. In the same way that he had earlier used theater to educate and enlighten his students in Lillehammer, he believed that theater and music could serve a beneficial purpose for the workers, cotters, and farmers of the labor associations. Because these views were so firmly ingrained in Thrane, when he took up the gavel of political activity a decade and a half later in Chicago, they became fundamental underpinnings of the first Norwegian ethnic theater in America.[9]

The political reaction that struck down the revolutions of 1848 on the continent also surfaced in Norway in reaction to the Thrane movement. In July 1851, Thrane and several other leaders of the movement were arrested and subsequently tried for what was considered to be revolutionary activity. Thrane served seven years in jail while his wife's health broke as she struggled to keep the family together. When he was finally released from prison in July 1858, Thrane found that his supporters had either emigrated or were afraid to associate with him. For a time, he traveled around the country as a photographer, but after his wife died in 1862, Thrane decided to follow the same advice he had given so many others seeking to escape the difficulties in Norway: he emigrated to America.

Leaving Norway in November 1863, Thrane and his four daughters arrived at Castle Garden on the southern tip of Manhattan Island on 2 February 1864. The family found cheap lodging in the Five Points District of New York. Getting established while the Civil War still raged proved a difficult matter. Prospects in New York were clearly difficult, because a year later when Thrane's son, Arthur, arrived he found his family living apart and described them as "poor, poor, poor."[10] Thrane had found some work as a writer and photographer for *Skandinavisk Post*, a Swedish newspaper in New York, but it was not until early 1866 that his life took a decisive turn when he accepted an invitation from a group of businessmen to move to Chicago and establish a newspaper there. In Chicago, he found people who fondly remembered the radical from Norway. The newspaper, it was hoped, would become a liberal competitor to the two existing newspapers, *Emigranten* and *Fædrelandet*, which, by and large, supported the

[9]Thrane, "Autobiographical Reminiscences," Marcus Thrane Papers; Oddvar Bjørklund, *Marcus Thrane,* 105, 130–141; Thrane, "Folke theater," in *Arbeiderforeningernes Blad*, 23 March 1850; Terje I. Leiren, *Marcus Thrane: A Norwegian Radical in America* (Northfield, Minnesota, 1987), 9–12.

[10]Arthur D. H. Thrane, "Reminiscences of the Late Dr. A. D. H. Thrane and Notes on Family," in *The Daily Telegram*, Eau Claire, Wisconsin, 18 June 1923; Vasilia Thrane Struck, "Marcus Thrane," Marcus Thrane Papers. For an excellent description of the perils of new immigrants in New York, see the firsthand account of Count Carl Lewenhaupt of the Norwegian-Swedish legation in Washington, D.C.: Paul A Vang, "Report of Count Carl Lewenhaupt on Swedish-American Immigration in 1870," *Swedish Pioneer Historical Quarterly* 30 (1979), 5–24.

Norwegian-American clergy. The business community wanted an alternative voice, but probably did not realize just how strident that voice would be. The paper, *Marcus Thrane's Norske Amerikaner*, first published on 25 May 1866, survived only four months. In that time, however, it channeled Thrane's energy and came to define his mission in America. That mission led Thrane to focus on political reform and to use the paper to try to build an organizational structure similar to his labor associations in Norway, but subsequently redirected him to emphasize cultural enlightenment which, initially, meant establishing the Norwegian Theater in Chicago.

In various articles in the *Norske Amerikaner*, Thrane told of his plans to organize Norwegian immigrants in the hopes of breaking what he considered to be the repressive grip of the Lutheran clergy. In his desire to enlighten his fellow Norwegian immigrants, he proposed the establishment of hospitals, immigrant aid associations, employment offices, singing associations, music groups, gun clubs, libraries, and political associations. On 11 June 1866, the founding meeting of *Den musikalske Forening* [The Musical Association] was held. In actuality, the Musical Association was an offshoot of the Thrane family's get-togethers, but its organization widened the circle and helped contribute to the subsequent building of a theatrical repertoire.[11]

Vehemently attacked by the Norwegian Synod for his criticism of organized religion, Thrane saw support for his paper dwindle as ordinary immigrants, feeling the pressure from their clergy, began to abandon the paper. As a result, he decided to sell the paper. The subscription list was sold to another new, but less political paper, *Skandinaven*, edited by his friend Knut Langeland. In announcing the sale, Thrane wrote that he would return with a new publication that would confront the clergy directly.[12] In essence, Thrane had concluded that most Norwegian-Americans were not yet ready to follow him in throwing off the shackles of the clergy. He had, naively perhaps, believed that the new country with its republican constitution would make a new and more enlightened per-

[11]Arthur D. H. Thrane, "Reminiscences," in *The Daily Telegram*, 18 June 1923; Marcus Thrane, "Det Norske Præsteveldet i Amerika," *Marcus Thranes Norske Amerikaner,* 15, 22 June 1866. For a full discussion of Thrane's newspaper, see Terje I. Leiren, "The Reemergence of a Misunderstood Radical: *Marcus Thranes Norske Amerikaner*," in *Scandinavians and Other Immigrants in Urban America: The Proceedings of a Research Conference*, edited by Odd Lovoll (Northfield, Minnesota, 1985), 111–122.

[12]Thrane, "Til den *Norske-Amerikaners* Abonnenter," *Skandinaven*, 13 September 1866. See also Arthur D. H. Thrane, "Reminiscences," in *The Daily Telegram*, 18 June 1923.

son out of the Norwegian farmer. The reality, he found out, was something quite different. Thrane came to recognize that "enlightenment" had not progressed as far as he had thought. Consequently, he had to look for other ways to get his message across, to enlighten and to educate the people.

Thrane remained convinced that newspapers were an important medium of communication. Public appearances took him directly to the people themselves and that too would continue to be an important means of communication. However, with his background and training in music and the theater, it was perhaps most natural for Marcus Thrane to turn to the theater as the preferred means of communicating his political message to the people. The theater could be friendly and nonthreatening; it could also be intellectually stimulating and culturally uplifting. Thrane understood that, while theater can entertain, it can also seduce. If the Norwegians in America were not ready for Thrane's political message delivered directly through the press or in his speeches, perhaps they would accept the message put into the context of an evening of entertainment.

One way or another, Thrane believed he would get his message out. If he couldn't convince the overwhelming number of Norwegians in America to join him, he might at least enlighten the few. With the Norwegian Theater, he could do so more gently, and by using his children and family friends as members of the troupe he could also satisfy his own longing for a profitable activity that would be a family venture.[13] Although Thrane's Norwegian Theater in Chicago survived less than two years, he continued his interest in theater by sporadically writing plays until he retired from public life in 1884. The final production of a Thrane play was a benefit performance in Chicago of *The Power of the Black Book* on 31 May 1884. Playwright and musician that he was, Thrane was, however, best known by his contemporaries and remembered most by posterity as a political radical. Arriving from Norway during the Civil War, in the United States Marcus Thrane would come to edit two newspapers and travel extensively, especially around the Midwest, speaking against what he considered the tyranny of organized religion, especially the Norwegian-American clergy, and as an advocate for free thought and intellectual enlightenment. These issues also come through in Thrane's plays, perhaps most successfully in *The Hypocrites* and *Holden*, both written after the Norwegian Theater in Chicago had ceased to exist.

[13]Thrane, "Til den *Norske-Amerikaners* Abonnenter," *Skandinaven*, 13 September 1866.

A trial appearance of Thrane's Norwegian Theater took place on the evening of 6 September 1866, at the German Hall on the corner of Wells and Indiana (now Grand Avenue) streets in Chicago. The program, beginning at 8 pm, included a concert by the Musical Society and the performance of a one-act play, *Abekatten* [*The Monkey*]. The evening concluded with a dance. The "Monkey" would become one of the popular mainstays of the Norwegian ethnic theater not only in Chicago, but in places like Minneapolis as well. It was, according to the prominent Minnesota Norwegian-American Carl G. O. Hansen, also performed at the opening of Normanna Hall in Minneapolis on 17 May 1889.[14]

On 13 September 1866, Thrane used the pages of *Skandinaven* to announce the demise of his newspaper, *Marcus Thranes Norske Amerikaner*. In the same issue, there also appeared a notice that a program introducing a new comedy would be presented by the *Norsk Theater* [Norwegian Theater] at the end of September.[15] The end of September came and went without a play, however, and on October 4, there was a new announcement that the play *Doktor mod Doktor* [*Doctor vs. Doctor*] would be presented on October 15. As usual, the play would be followed by a social evening with dancing until long past midnight. The delay was most likely caused by the need to ready the script and the actors, to print tickets, posters, and notices, as well as to acquire the numerous props that Thrane called for.[16]

The play is a standard comedy that deals with the competition for the hand of an heiress by two doctors, one young and favored by the woman, and one old, wealthy, and foolish, favored by her hypochondriac father. No review of the play from October 15 appears to have been printed, but when it was performed by Thrane's troupe a year later it received a descriptive review in *Svenska Amerikanaren* suggesting that it did not excite anyone. The play lacks any local color and has no features that would distinguish it as an immigrant play. As an initial effort, however, it appears to have been successful entertainment.[17]

[14]*Marcus Thranes Norske Amerikaner*, 31 August 1866; Carl G. O. Hansen, *My Minneapolis* (Minneapolis, 1956), 144.

[15]*Skandinaven*, 13 September 1866.

[16]*Skandinaven*, 4 October 1866. The title of the play, *Doktor mod Doktor*, was written with a "k" in the advertisements, but Thrane wrote it with a "c" on his manuscript.

[17]*Svenska Amerikanaren*, 6 November 1867. The manuscript of the play is in the Marcus Thrane Papers of the National Library, Oslo. I have chosen not to include it in this collection because, apart from being the first Thrane play performed, it lacks any special features that make it particularly significant in the context of the Thrane's authorship of Norwegian-American drama.

The second effort by the small troupe deserves particular notice because the play, *Det uskikkelige pigebarn* [*The Naughty Girl*], featured Thrane's daughter Vasilia in the lead role. Not until its third performance in the summer of 1867, however, was the play reviewed and then the review consisted primarily of comments on the acting skills of Vasilia, who had clearly become an audience favorite among Chicago's Scandinavians. Undoubtedly on the strength of her performances in her father's plays, she was invited to join the English-language McVicker's Theater in Chicago, where she made her debut on 26 October 1867 in a play titled *Our Country Cousin*. In reviewing the play, the *Chicago Tribune* praised her as "pretty, petite, and graceful," but criticized her for being "nervous and embarrassed."[18] Nevertheless, it was a significant tribute to her acting skills, and the abilities of the amateur actors in Thrane's company, that they would be invited to join larger English-language productions while continuing to perform at the ethnic theater. In addition to Vasilia, two other of Thrane's children, Camilla and Arthur, also performed in the productions, and it was in this milieu that all three met their future spouses. It was not an unproductive time for the Thrane family.

On 15 November 1866, a letter appeared in *Skandinaven* that praised the first two efforts of the Norwegian Theater and called on the Scandinavian communities to support the effort: "It is with true pleasure that we observe the many small traces which recently appear of the progress of enlightenment and cultivated society among our countrymen here, and as one of these we permit ourselves to point out the newly established National Theater." The letter went on to note that, although there were points to criticize, the actors were genuinely talented with abilities that exceeded expectations and held considerable promise for the future. After calling for more "genuine Norwegian plays," the letter concluded with the appeal to encourage "the little step forward on the path of culture and show other nationalities that there also exists among Scandinavians a taste for the beautiful."[19]

The troupe did indeed perform several plays that can be said to be "genuine Norwegian plays." Among these was the extremely popular *Til Sæters* [*To the Mountain Farm*] by C. P. Riis, that was set in the spectacular Norwegian countryside and told the story of a group of students going off to a mountain farm to convince a farmer not to emigrate to America. This one-act play, filled with National Romantic images, was extremely popular in Norway at the time Thrane's political activity was at its

[18]*Chicago Tribune*, 27, 28 October 1867; *Svenska Amerikanaren*, 6 November 1867.

[19]*Skandinaven*, 15 November 1866.

height. Another play with less obvious National Romantic overtones was *Ervingen* [*The Heir*] by Ivar Aasen. With a standard vaudevillian theme of love triumphant, the play became a favorite for its use of folk melodies and perhaps also because it was written in the western Norwegian *landsmaal* form of Norwegian, which Aasen had developed as a national linguistic countermeasure to the Danish-Norwegian literary language used by a majority of Norwegians, including the nation's elite. It appears most likely that Thrane knew about the letter to *Skandinaven* praising the Norwegian Theater, or it may be that he was the letter writer, because both *Ervingen* and *Til Sæters* were produced by his Norwegian Theater before the end of 1866. *Ervingen* was performed on November 21 and *Til Sæters* around Christmas.[20]

The obvious popularity of national themes no doubt also encouraged Thrane to write plays to fit that interest. Two such were *Gjæst Baardsen* and *Syttende Mai* [*The Seventeenth of May*]. The manuscripts of both plays have been lost, but reviews of the performances provide some information about them. The historical *Gjæst Baardsen*, who died in 1849, achieved considerable fame and notoriety in early nineteenth-century Norway for his Robin Hood-like exploits and legendary escapes from captivity. It is easy to understand that the immigrants, many of whom came from the lower classes in Norway, sympathized with Baardsen as they idealized his exploits. The play was first performed on 8 April 1867, with Thrane's twenty-year-old son, Arthur, in the role of Baardsen.

Arthur also played the lead in *Syttende Mai*, a two-act "national song piece" that was extensively reviewed in *Skandinaven* and *Emigranten*. In addition to Arthur, Camilla and Vasilia appeared in this play, which premiered on 17 May 1867, Norway's national holiday and anniversary of the Norwegian Constitution of 1814. The first act takes place in Norway and focuses on Nils Sundløkka, a cotter working for a wealthy farmer named Eriksen. Sundløkka wants to celebrate the Norwegian Constitution by taking the day off from work. Eriksen rejects his request, ordering him to work as usual. Failing to understand why he can not get the day off, Nils is supported by his son, Iver, and daughter, Birthe. His wife, Kari, however, is fearful that his attitude will cause trouble that may lead to the

[20]A letter from Chicago to Drammen, Norway, dated 27 December 1866, published in *Drammens Tidende* on 4 March 1867, was sent to someone who obviously knew Thrane from his days in Drammen. The writer was a person who had seen *Til Sæters* a few days earlier. The writer notes that the play was a Thrane family production and included another acquaintance, Hans Struck, an architect. The letter stated that Thrane and Struck "have their sons and daughters with them, making eight in number, and are doing well." See *Drammens Tidende*, 4 March 1867.

family being evicted from the farm. She advises him to give in. Thrane probably modeled Kari from personal experience, since his wife, Josephine, had counseled moderation during his own political activity in Norway. But, as Thrane had in real life, Nils rejects the advice, drinking a toast to Norwegian freedom. This infuriates Eriksen, who takes revenge by denying Nils's son, Iver, the hand of his daughter in marriage. Heartbroken, Iver decides to emigrate to America, claiming he will become rich there and eventually return to marry his Marthe. Nils, who had always denounced emigration as a loss for Norway, also decides to emigrate to America.

In Act II of *Syttende Mai*, the family is in America. Nils has become a prosperous Minnesota farmer with fancy clothes. His wife and daughter have assumed the appearance of Yankees in style and dress. Iver still misses Marthe, but his letters to her have not been answered. He hears rumors that she has married someone else. As a result, Birthe tries to arrange a union between her brother and her American friend, Miss Clark, but Iver is not interested. Meanwhile, back in Norway, Marthe had not married anyone else, but had remained true to Iver. Now she arrives from Norway, looking for him. Also entering the picture is a seminary student, Olsen, who had proposed to Birthe in Act I, but had been rejected because he could not dance. The church frowned on dancing and no self-respecting seminary student would jeopardize his career by learning to dance. But, in America, that had changed. Now he had learned to dance: "For your sake, Birthe, I have become a heathen! For your sake, I have learned to dance." It was not enough, however, for Birthe wanted to marry a real American. The seminary student, interestingly enough, finds solace with Miss Clark, while Iver and Marthe marry each other.[21]

Reviews of the play praised the actors. Arthur, according to *Skandinaven*, had a "first-rate aptitude for the stage," where he performed with "an ease and unforced naturalness" that gave "an absolutely favorable impression."[22] The play, however, was less enthusiastically received, largely because of the subtle political message, which *Skandinaven*'s reviewer chose to interpret positively. The play, it was noted, gave a negative view of Norwegian freedom, but added that: "We must, nevertheless, deduce that it was not the shortcomings of the Constitution but rather its misuse or non-use that the author wanted to criticize."[23]

A far less benign view of the play and its author appeared in *Emigranten*, one of the Chicago papers that regularly sided with the Norwegian

[21]*Skandinaven*, 23 May 1867; *Emigranten*, 25 May 1867.
[22]*Skandinaven*, 23 May 1867.
[23]*Skandinaven*, 23 May 1867.

clergy in its criticism of Thrane. The paper's editor, Carl Frederik Solberg, wrote that he found the play unnecessarily "full of points of indictment against the old mother country," and was most irritated by Thrane using Norway's national holiday to write a "protest petition against Norway."[24] Solberg was also irritated by the use of profanity by Nils in the first act, claiming that a person can be poor without being ungodly. He also found the portrayal of the seminary student to be unfair and distorted. Solberg, however, appears to have been most infuriated by Thrane himself. Solberg wrote:

> After having seen Marcus Thrane as a popular leader in Norway and as an editor in America, we have now seen him as a people's educator through the theater. We must say that he is equally unfortunate, equally incompetent, in all three roles. Among his previous followers we have met many good minds, here in Chicago and elsewhere, who could raise real sympathy for the cause he pretended to lead. It was the misfortune of these friends of reform—and there was indeed need for reform—that they got such an incompetent leader. Now he pursues them in America and insists that they should support him by buying the same old hysterical, immature opinions which he peddles in small doses in the form of lectures, plays, and so on. It is poisonous feed. There are many Thrane-ites who under the better and freer conditions here have become more capable of leading his former followers than he is. It would be better for them to raise a small sum for his support and be rid of him. There is no Norwegian cotter class in America and a Marcus Thrane is not worth the money he is paid.[25]

Syttende Mai was performed a second time on 12 August 1867, in connection with a benefit picnic for the Scandinavian emigrant fund. The picnic was reported to be a huge success with 1,200 participants representing Danish, Norwegian, and Swedish groups. The play was performed in spite of rainy weather and half the proceeds were donated by Thrane to the Emigrant Aid Society. That over a thousand people would show up to view a Thrane play suggests that, although Solberg may have spoken for many, he did not represent all the Scandinavian immigrants in Chicago.[26]

[24]*Emigranten*, 25 May 1867.

[25]Carl Frederik Solberg, in *Emigranten*, 25 May 1867. Solberg's attack on Thrane did not end with this statement. In addition, he attacked his integrity and honesty by claiming that Thrane had tried to profit by renting the Turner Hall with plans to rent it back to the "Nora Selskap" for their meeting. In response, Thrane challenged Solberg to a duel ("Either retract your insulting utterances or meet me in a duel with pistols," Thrane wrote). In the end, nothing came of the challenge, but it is clear that Thrane could take criticism of his plays, but was extremely sensitive to attacks he considered personal. See *Emigranten*, 17 June 1867.

[26]*Skandinaven*, 8, 15 August 1867; *Svenska Amerikanaren*, 14 August, 28 October, 1867.

If the immigrant theme is the central pillar in *Syttende Mai*, it is also the core of one of Thrane's best plays from this period, *En amerikansk tjenestepige* [*An American Servant Girl*], a one-act comedy that presents Thrane's views on class distinctions in a subtle and charming fashion. *An American Servant Girl* tells the story of the Brun family, upper-class urban immigrants from Norway, and their difficulty in adjusting to the less formal, more egalitarian, social styles of America. Their servant girl, on the other hand, finds America's egalitarian culture perfect for her tastes. Thrane presents the Americanized Norwegian servant girl, Dina, as the direct opposite of the stereotypical servant. She is self-confident, cultured, and delightfully obnoxious. Mr. Brun and his daughter, Cecilie, assume that Dina is unable to play the piano because, coming from a lower station of life, she has neither had the time to practice nor the money to pay for lessons. It is a false assumption, however, as Thrane makes clear. Class and wealth have nothing to do with whether or not someone has true culture.

It is through the character of Dina and her situation that Thrane makes most of his political points in the play, that culture is not the monopoly of the upper classes and that America's egalitarian society levels all. "Here in America, things are not done the way we were used to back home," says Dina. "Here a servant girl does just what pleases her, yes, some day even the right to vote may come."[27] The irony of the title is that Dina is not an American servant girl at all, but an Americanized Norwegian-American servant girl. But in contrast to the Bruns, she is presented as the appreciative beneficiary of American freedom and equality. Hence, in this entertaining one-act play, Thrane comments on the absurdity of cultural prejudices as well as the positive benefits of American society for European immigrants.

The situation Thrane builds on appears to have been biographical and based on the personal experiences of his own daughters. When the family first arrived in New York, economic circumstances forced Thrane to allow two of his daughters, Markitta and Vasilia, to take positions as servants. According to Vasilia: "One afternoon we were alone and Markitta started playing operatic music so that I might practice the dances taught me by Hr. Sorensen in Arendal. Unfortunately these included LaCachucca; in our ecstasy we did not hear the carriage drive in. . . . we were led to understand that our accomplishments were of a dangerous character."[28] That

[27]Thrane, *En amerikansk tjenestepige*, Ms. 4° 1768a–b, in Marcus Thrane Papers, National Library, Oslo.

[28]Vasilia Struck, "Marcus Thrane, " in Marcus Thrane Papers, National Library, Oslo.

Vasilia played the part of Dina in the play was, perhaps, an element of ironic revenge for the Thrane family.

The play that seems to have been the most popular of Thrane's plays with the Norwegian Theater was *Skydskiftet i Hallingdal* [*The Posting Station in Hallingdal*]. Performed four times between 11 February 1867 and 9 January 1868, it also appears to have held a special fascination for Marcus Thrane himself. That it held a special place in Thrane's own heart can also be surmised through his correspondence with his son, Arthur. In 1871, when Arthur was looking to establish his medical practice, Marcus invited his son to consider Chicago, stating that, while developing his practice, he could supplement his income by running an evening school. It was a natural assumption by Thrane himself that theater would be a part of the curriculum and that he would make *The Posting Station in Hallingdal* available to his son for that purpose. In a letter to Arthur, dated 24 September 1871, Marcus noted that he had added a song at the end of Act I because he thought the original ending too dull.[29]

The Posting Station in Hallingdal falls into the category of a rags-to-riches story. A young couple, Anders and Snefrid, are in love with each other, but face rejection by the girl's father because Anders has no money, property, or prospects. In his depression, Anders plans to emigrate to America where Snefrid is willing to join him. Emigration, however, becomes unnecessary when a wealthy English aristocrat arrives at the posting station looking for someone to guide him into the mountains to hunt. As his guide, Anders saves the Englishman's life by rescuing him from a ferocious bear and is rewarded with a huge gift that allows him to buy the land he wants and to marry Snefrid without having to emigrate to America.

While the plot presents a fairly standard love story, *The Posting Station* is most notable for its incorporation of a striking musical score and operatic songs. Unlike in his other plays, Thrane has written *The Posting Station* using the language of rural and western Norway. However, whether it was to show its cruder aspects or simply that Thrane was less familiar with it, the dialogue is peppered with grammatical errors. There is a kind of rustic charm in the dialogue and the bantering that gives it an exaggerated colloquial feel. The use or misuse of grammar, however, was not the only way Thrane broke new ground. In addition, Thrane includes an old woman who uses spells and concoctions to read fortunes and foretell the future. Guri is the old woman in this play who, in spite of being a

[29]Letter of Marcus Thrane to Arthur Thrane, 24 September 1871, in Marcus Thrane Papers, National Library, Oslo.

believer in and practitioner of magic, is presented as a particularly sympathetic character. In his speeches and his writings, Thrane may have railed against superstition and unscientific beliefs, but in his plays, he was clearly able to use the theme in a positive and generative fashion.

What is noble in *The Posting Station*, however, becomes superstition in *The Power of the Black Book*, when Thrane uses the theme again more than a decade later. It is clear that Thrane, in spite of his firm political and ideological views, could approach theme and story as an artist and not always as a political ideologue eager to make a political point. As a result, one is tempted to acknowledge that there is the sense of a true artist in Thrane's approach to theater and playwriting. He did not simply use theater as a tool to further a political message, but as a statement of art and culture that could also have a significant edifying function in addition to being didactic.

While the Norwegian Theater was Thrane's main source of income and his principal interest from 1866 to 1868, he was also involved in several other ventures, such as giving speeches or serving as special agent for the Inman Shipping Line. None of these ventures, however, proved particularly profitable for him. The theater troupe frequently resorted to special benefit performances for the actors or for Thrane himself. That he survived was, to a great extent, due to his spartan lifestyle, but also that he was aided by his children. They were, however, beginning to move their own lives in independent directions. Arthur set up a medical practice, married, and began to raise a family. Marcus, however, remained dependent on his son's generosity from time to time to provide him money for clothing as well as occasional tickets to special events. In one instance, in 1879, Thrane attended a performance of Gilbert and Sullivan's *H.M.S. Pinafore*.[30] He was obviously enthralled by the musical because less than a year later Thrane would incorporate melodies from the production into one of his most important plays, *Holden*.

Because his children were beginning to go in independent directions, and because he wanted to get back into the newspaper business to pursue his unfinished crusade against the Norwegian clergy, Thrane decided to close the Norwegian Theater in early 1868. On 12 March 1868, the remnants of the company joined a new venture with greater ambitions and the hope of greater public support as well, the Norwegian Dramatic Society [*Den Norske Dramatisk Forening*].[31] Although Thrane ended his di-

[30]Letter of Marcus Thrane to Arthur Thrane, 29 April 1879, in Marcus Thrane Papers, National Library, Oslo.

[31]The Norwegian Dramatic Society presented plays from 1868 to 1872 and included most of the actors originally organized by Thrane. In addition to some of the plays authored

rect association with the theater when the Norwegian Dramatic Society was organized, the new group still performed some of Thrane's popular plays and many of the same names appear as actors in the plays—Elise Struck, Vasilia Thrane, Frank Wærness, E. S. Howland, among others. Like Thrane's Norwegian Theater, the Norwegian Dramatic Society also performed popular plays from Scandinavia. In their 1938 study of the Dramatic Society, Napier Wilt and Henrietta Naeseth showed how closely the repertoire of the Chicago theaters and the new national theater in Bergen, Norway, were coordinated. That the founder of the *National Scene* [National Theater] in Bergen, Ole Bull, had connections with the Dramatic Society when he was in Chicago, further speaks to the interplay between the ethnic immigrant theater and the national theater of Norway.[32]

In welcoming the Dramatic Society, *Skandinaven* indicated that the organizers were expected to be more altruistic than Thrane had been. The bylaws for the Norwegian Dramatic Society included a stipulation that the profits were to be used exclusively for worthy ends. It proved to be good publicity, but not necessarily philanthropic, since the income for the society was never particularly noteworthy. As if to take a final swipe at Thrane's National Theater, *Skandinaven,* in its first review of the new company on 2 April 1868, praised the actors for knowing their roles: something, it noted, that had not always been the case with the earlier company.[33] There is no record of a response from Thrane. If the back-handed compliment hurt him, it went unrecorded. In the Spring of 1868, Thrane moved back into a politically active life where theater was less central. As he began to publish a Freethinker monthly, *Dagslyset*, his interest in theater was, however, neither forgotten nor abandoned. In fact, it was not unlikely that theater became, for Thrane in these years, increasingly important as a special opportunity to make a political statement. In the years to come, there would be several opportunities. The first one came in late 1871 in the wake of the great Chicago fire.

In the years immediately after leaving the Norwegian Theater, Thrane focused his efforts on the publication of *Dagslyset*, a spirited, analytical newspaper with a radical anticlerical bias. Its platform included the

---

by Thrane, the society expanded its repertoire to include a broader range of productions. See Napier Wilt and Henrietta C. Koren Naeseth, "Two Early Norwegian Dramatic Societies in Chicago," *Norwegian-American Studies and Records* (Northfield, MN, 1938) 10:50–52.

[32]The repertoire of Thrane's theater as well as of its successor is strikingly similar to that of the Bergen theater, except that Thrane used more of his own plays. See Wilt and Naeseth, "Two Early Norwegian Dramatic Societies in Chicago," *Norwegian-American Studies and Records* (1938).

[33]*Skandinaven*, 19 March, 2 April, 1868.

elimination of the power and prestige of the clergy while enlightening the Norwegian immigrant on the benefits of republican democracy, socialism, and scientific progress. Biblical criticism and references to Darwin's *Origin of Species* were common topics, but most frequently *Dagslyset* advocated Freethinking and its opposition to religious and political orthodoxy. Increasingly, Thrane and his newspaper became associated with the Chicago Society of Progress founded in June 1869. As its first secretary, Thrane was closely involved and the most visible public figure. Some of the most prominent Scandinavians in Chicago were either members or supporters of the society. Members included Dr. Gerhard Paoli, a prominent physician and first president of the society; Iver Lawson, founder of the *Chicago Daily News*; Carl F. Peterson, editor of the Swedish-language newspaper *Nya Världen*; and Jacob Johnson, a wealthy businessman.[34] Every January 29, the society would celebrate the birthday of its "patron saint," the American and French revolutionary hero and radical Freethinker Thomas Paine, author of the influential 1776 pamphlet, *Common Sense*. It was not a widely popular celebration. In her three-volume history of Chicago, Bessie Louise Pierce noted that religious dissenters in Chicago were ostracized by society in general. "Freethinkers," she wrote, "received the heaviest condemnation of all. No greater reproach could be directed against a man than to call him infidel, agnostic, atheist. Into such unsavory company were cast all who admired the works of Thomas Paine and who indulged in the celebration of his birthday."[35] In such company Marcus Thrane publicly reveled and while he may not have benefited either socially or financially, he gained a great deal of personal satisfaction in the belief that his cause was just and would, in the long run, prove victorious. So, for the Paine birthday celebration, Thrane wrote a one-act play, *The Hypocrites or Love during the Fire*, using the recent traumatic Chicago fire of October 1871 as the setting.

The great Chicago fire began on 8 October 1871. Raging for several days, it devastated the city and is claimed by historian Odd Lovoll to have been "one of the most spectacular events" in America in the nineteenth century. It killed more than 300 people and left one third of the city's population homeless. Six Scandinavian churches were destroyed, including the newly built and recently dedicated Swedish Immanuel Church on Sedgewick Street. Inner-city missionary activity abounded in the wake of the fire as clerics emphasized the wrath of God toward a populace in des-

[34]*Dagslyset*, November 1869, January 1870.

[35]Bessie Louise Pierce, *From Town to City, 1848–1871*, vol. 2 of *A History of Chicago* (New York, 1957), 381, 182.

perate need of conversion and religious revival.[36] The cause of the fire became a matter of considerable debate that Thrane subsequently used to great effect in his personal correspondence, in an essay in *Dagslyset*, in his *Wisconsin Bible* (a mock biblical satire on the Norwegian synod), and in his play *The Hypocrites*.

Thrane's personal correspondence shows he was initially traumatized by the fire and its devastation. Once over that, however, he ridiculed the idea that God's avenging finger had been pointed at Chicago and that the fire had been a result of his wrath. Writing in *Dagslyset,* Thrane pointed out that if God was punishing the ungodly, he had an strange way of doing it. He noted that "whereas 55 churches burned, Freethinkers remained remarkably untouched—among Scandinavians, the strongest supporters of the Bible, namely the Swedes, were the worst affected. Most of them lived on the north side, which went completely up in smoke. Norwegians, on the other hand, who are less religious, and the Danes, who refuse to support even one minister, for the most part were spared."[37]

As one would expect, the play paints an extremely positive picture of the Freethinker protagonist, whom Thrane gave the ironic, but symbolic, name of Christian. To the wealthy, pious, and hypocritical couple who give the play its title, Thrane gave equally ironic names, Mr. and Mrs. Pious ("*From*" in Norwegian). A superstitious, uneducated servant of the From family is called Mikkel. Like the biblical archangel, Mikkel is the play's messenger who runs in and out of the action, bringing news of the fire outside while shouting warnings about the pyromaniacal Freethinkers and communists. As the play reaches its climax, Mikkel hides under a table (in allusion to the Archangel Michael's association with caves?) in an attempt to escape the Freethinkers, if not the fire. In spite of the imagery surrounding the names, the story Thrane tells is simple and direct. Christian, the Freethinker, is in love with Caroline, the daughter of Mr. and Mrs. From, who reject him as a suitor because he is a Freethinker. However, when Mr. From believes that the fire has destroyed his business, and with it all his money and papers, Christian shows up with his arms filled with papers, protocols, and cash that he has saved from the fire. Thrane's moral: the Freethinker is the "real" Christian and, in gratitude, Christian and Caroline are allowed to marry.

[36]Odd S. Lovoll, *A Century of Urban Life: The Norwegians in Chicago before 1930* (Northfield, Minnesota, 1988), 107–108).

[37]Thrane, "Chicago Brand og Guds Finger," in *Dagslyset*, January 1872. Thrane's initial shock and his observations of the devastation can be seen in his correspondence with his son. See Letters of Marcus Thrane to Arthur Thrane, 10, 15 October 1871, in Marcus Thrane Papers, National Library, Oslo.

In this case, the Chicago fire and the celebrations of Thomas Paine combined to give Thrane the opportunity to return to the theater with a new play, but generally he was too busy with *Dagslyset* to commit any significant time to play writing. It appears that dramatic and musical evenings remained a part of his social life in Chicago and, whenever he could, he attended theatrical performances whether they were ethnic Scandinavian theater or the mainstream English-language theater.

The years Thrane edited *Dagslyset* were among his busiest. In addition to editing the paper and writing most of the material it published, Thrane gave numerous lectures and traveled extensively, including a trip to Denver, Colorado. Probably because of his position as an editor, he maintained an intense interest in national and regional political activity, including presidential politics and the rise of international socialism. The Grange and Knights of Labor movements fascinated him and may well have reminded him of his own activity in Norway more than twenty years before. Throughout the decade of the 1870s, even with his often frantic activity, *Dagslyset* never showed any real financial success. It frustrated Thrane to the extent that he lashed out at his readers in January 1878, when, like a spoiled child, he refused to wish his readers a happy new year, calling Scandinavians in America "lazy, indifferent, and egotistical."[38] It was a diatribe that did him no honor. In his personal correspondence following the end of *Dagslyset,* Thrane appeared resigned to a less active life. Nevertheless, the end of *Dagslyset,* in February 1878, brought Thrane to one of the lowest emotional points he experienced in America. He had passed his sixtieth birthday and probably felt the weight of the years as much physically as he did emotionally. As a new decade opened in 1880, however, events again propelled Thrane into a fury of activity and ushered in an exceptionally productive time in his life. From early 1880 until the end of 1884, Marcus Thrane wrote several plays, completed his *Wisconsin Bible,* traveled extensively in support of bringing new immigrants to the Upper Midwest, especially the Red River Valley, and he took a nostalgic trip back to Europe where he visited England, France, Germany, Denmark and, finally, Norway. The spark of renewal came from a most unlikely and unexpected source, but it was a spark Thrane nursed and protected until it grew into a regenerating fire that may well have left him feeling like a new phoenix rising. The spark was a church scandal. Could Thrane have wished for anything better?

In January 1880, *Skandinaven* carried an account from *Budstikken,* a Norwegian-language paper in Minneapolis, that one of the most promi-

[38]Thrane, "Nytaar," *Dagslyset,* January 1878.

nent ministers in the Norwegian Lutheran Church, Bernt Julius Muus, had for years mistreated, neglected, and abused his wife. Oline Muus sued for divorce and retained the prominent Minneapolis lawyer Andreas Ueland to represent her. Following the death of her father in 1862, Oline had inherited $4,000. Norwegian law gave her husband the right of disposition and Oline apparently never saw the money. Divorce-court testimony also revealed that Muus had denied his wife and children basic creature comforts in their home and that he did not allow them medical treatment when needed. In 1877, after Oline broke her leg, Muus reportedly refused to call a doctor and denied her the use of a horse to get help. A neighbor finally intervened and summoned a doctor, but Muus refused his wife a crutch. Although he may appear to have been simply unfeeling and callous, Muus appealed to the authority of the scriptures and traditional mores to claim the right of a husband to rule over his wife and family.[39] Be that as it may, the Muus affair was confirmation of what Thrane had been arguing for years, that the Norwegian-American clergy were arrogant, vindictive, mean, and un-Christian in their dealings with their families as well as their parishioners. For three months in the beginning of 1880, the scandal unfolded and Thrane took up his pen to write another comedy. *Holden* was ready by early June.

Taking liberty with the actual facts of the case, *Holden* tells the story of Bernt's authoritarian rule over his parishioners in Holden parish and over his family. Having only recently enjoyed the Gilbert and Sullivan opera *H.M.S. Pinafore* when it played in Chicago in the previous April, Thrane borrowed several melodies from that musical and incorporated them into his "synod opera" in much the same way a folk singer will put new words to an old and familiar tune. In the play itself, Oline increasingly asserts her rights and her independence as she understands them. She demands her money and, finally, a divorce to end her suffering. Bernt, appealing to the authority of scripture, argues the traditional role for himself as husband and father to make all decisions, which the wife must obey. The sympathetic portrayal of Oline Muus by Thrane is consistent with his progressive views on equality in marriage and the rights of

[39]*Skandinaven*, 22, 27 January; 9, 30 March 1880. Oline Muus filed suit in 1879 for control of the $4000 inheritance from her father, alleging abuse and neglect against her husband, Bemt Muus. A study of the civil and ecclesiastical court cases as well as the newspaper coverage of the "Muus affair" is presented in Kathryn Ericson, "Triple Jeopardy: The Muus vs. Muus Case in Three Forums," *Minnesota History* 50 (Winter 1987) 298–308. Joseph M. Shaw, *Bernt Julius Muus: Founder of St. Olaf College* (Northfield, MN: Norwegian-American Historical Association, 1999) gives an objective overview of the scandal. Oline's young lawyer, Andreas Ueland, discusses the case briefly in *Recollections of An Immigrant* (New York: Minton, Balch and Co., 1929), 42.

women, which he professed in his speeches and essays as well as in his drama. Being the father of four daughters undoubtedly influenced Thrane's exceptionally liberal view for that time.

A review of the premier performance of the play, which appeared in *Skandinaven* and which Thrane kept among his papers, tells of an exceptional evening of theater. The Aurora Turner Hall was packed with an audience that saw a performance that exceeded all expectations. According to the review: "Except for a few glitches in the less significant roles, the performance was as smooth as butter. It is not often that a play flows this smoothly on a Scandinavian stage." The reviewer noted the borrowed melodies and praised the actors. He told of an evening of unstoppable laughter and storming applause for the performers, but also for Marcus Thrane, the play's author, who was called to the stage with a boisterous curtain call.[40]

No doubt encouraged by the response to *Holden*, Thrane was also inspired by a visit to America by Norwegian writer Bjørnstjerne Bjørnson from December 1880 to April 1881. Thrane sat in the audience to hear Bjørnson's final speech in the Aurora Turner Hall on 9 April 1881, and he reveled in the criticism of religious orthodoxy. When Bjørnson left to return to Norway, Thrane wrote that "the whole of Vesterheimen set up a howl like a pack of dogs," clearly delighted at the discomfort that Bjørnson had created among the Norwegian-Americans. Subsequently, the Chicago fire, the Muus affair, and Bjørnson's visit to Norwegian America all became part of the satirical *Wisconsin Bible* that Thrane finished around this time, further embellishing his reputation as a blasphemer.[41]

By the end of 1882, arrangements were in place for Thrane's long-planned trip back to Europe and, especially, Norway. It was intended to be a nostalgic return for which the Thingvalla Line and the Nickel Plate Railroad provided some funds, in addition to money from small fees for lecturing that Thrane had been able to set aside. His return to Norway was advertised as an excursion for which the Thingvalla Line was able to sell several hundred tickets to immigrants who wished to accompany Thrane on the trans-Atlantic crossing.

[40]"Den norske Synode-Opera," review of *Holden*, June 1880, copy in Marcus Thrane Papers, National Library, Oslo.

[41]Marcus Thrane, *Den Gamle Wisconsin-Bibelen* (Minneapolis, 1908). An English translation by Thrane's granddaughter, Linsie Caroline Krook, and F. Hilding Krook, of New Ulm, Minnesota, was made in 1955 and is in the archives of the Norwegian-American Historical Association. Chapters 10–14, which deal with Bjørnson's visit, are also published in Eva Lund Haugen and Einar Haugen, *Land of the Free: Bjørnstjerne Bjørnson's America Letters, 1880–1881* (Northfield, Minnesota, 1978), 266–277. Also see Frank G. Nelson, "Marcus Thrane og den gamle Wisconsin-bibelen," *Dagbladet*, 28 December 1948.

In Europe, Thrane spent five weeks in Copenhagen, five weeks in London, a week in Paris, five days in Berlin, and three months in Norway. He visited numerous relatives, including his brother and sister, who still lived in Oslo. In lectures he discussed America's light and dark sides and told about his new life. The fear his name continued to instill in many Norwegians resulted in his being refused the rental of the Labor Society Hall for a speech. Most of his time in Europe was spent, according to his own diary, attending musical performances and theater productions. On April 1, for example, he saw Henrik Ibsen's *Enemy of the People*. If he did not think of himself as the real Dr. Stockman, he understood that for many in Norway, even after thirty years, he was still "an enemy of the privileged people."[42]

When he returned to America aboard the *City of Berlin* from Liverpool, Thrane wrote two plays, several poems, and the monologue *The European Soldier*. He was tired and disillusioned, perhaps even bitter. He had believed that he would be remembered fondly by his former followers if not by the establishment, but that was not to be. His arrival in Norway had coincided with an intense conflict over the interpretation of the King's right of veto under the constitution. Thrane's appearance frightened the government, which thought he had come to agitate for a republic. In reality, his trip was made almost exclusively for personal reasons—to see his family after two decades, to visit the old country, and perhaps to gain a measure of respect that had been denied him before he left.

Back home in Chicago, Thrane was not quite ready to give up. He helped to organize a program which, it turned out, was a farewell to his friends and supporters. On 31 May 1884, the final theater and dance arranged by Thrane was held. There is no record of how large an audience attended, but in a subsequent letter to his son, Arthur, Marcus wrote that he lost money on the venture. He also acknowledged that he was tired and, at sixty-six years of age, feeling old.[43] Arthur, an established physician in Eau Claire, Wisconsin, invited his father to come live with him. Thrane left Chicago for the last time on 23 August 1884. He moved in with Arthur and his family, taking a small room on the second floor. There he lived for the next six years. Although he did receive occasional visitors, he became a full-time grandfather, a role he probably cherished more than anything else he had done in his life.

[42]Marcus Thrane, from Chicago to Norway, Ms. 4° 1781:1, Marcus Thrane Papers, National Library, Oslo.

[43]Letters of Marcus Thrane to Arthur Thrane,12, 22 August 1884, in Marcus Thrane Papers, National Library, Oslo.

When he died on 30 April 1890, the family held a simple burial in Lakeview Cemetery in Eau Claire. In Chicago, on June 1, Thrane's old comrades and friends celebrated his life with a stirring memorial service. His family kept his personal papers, and left to us his readers a few letters, some pictures, copies of his newspaper, *Dagslyset*, and most of his plays.[44]

[44]Kept by Thrane's descendents until the 1960s, the handwritten manuscripts of most of Thrane's surviving plays were deposited in the Norwegian National Library archives in Oslo. One play, *Dannelse fremfor alt*, is located in the University of Bergen Library.

An American Servant Girl

A COMEDY IN ONE ACT

Characters:

MR. BRUN

CECILIE, his daughter

DINA, the servant girl

PETERSEN

MILLER, a Musician

A POSTMAN

Stage:
A furnished living room with a piano on the right. On the left is a table and a mirror. There is a door in the background and a door to the left.

Scene 1: CECILIE and DINA

CECILIE *(seated at piano, playing and singing)*

DINA *(enters during the song, dusting the furniture; she listens to the song, then mimics Cecilie by pretending to play on the table)* That is a beautiful song! Oh! How pretty it is!

CECILIE *(to herself)* Uff! Why does this impudent servant girl always have to be underfoot?

DINA You sing beautifully, Miss. I have heard nightingales trill in the twilight of the summer night, but never—

CECILIE *(with a commanding expression)* Oh, please spare me your flattery. Go to the kitchen and tend to your work!

DINA Oh, don't worry, I will take care of my work. When I heard you sing this pretty song, heaven help me, I had to come up for a moment. Tell me, Miss: Is it very expensive to learn to play the piano?

CECILIE Yes, it is very expensive.

DINA How expensive is it, approximately?

CECILIE Certainly more than you can afford.

DINA Don't say that. I have saved forty dollars, and I thought you might teach me.

CECILIE It is not proper for a servant girl to play the piano.

DINA I know that it isn't proper in Europe, but it's another matter here in America—for we are in a free country, you know.

CECILIE *(aside)* A free country! Yes, a wonderful country! God grant that I were far from here.

DINA You seem upset.

CECILIE What does that have to do with you?

DINA It has everything to do with me. Isn't it the duty of a servant girl to be interested in everything that happens in the house? I often see you sad and can't help but feel that you are unhappy.

CECILIE Well? And so what?

DINA But, my God, your father has such a good position.

CECILIE *(to herself)* Yes, and on his way to bankruptcy.

DINA But he has a factory, and that's not bad here in America.

CECILIE Oh, here in America and here in America. You're always coming with your "here in America." I only wish I was far away from America.

DINA But, why did you come then?

CECILIE Well, it certainly wasn't my idea.

DINA That may be, but it is well known that your father decided to leave the old country because he could not make it.

CECILIE Listen here, Dina, I am telling you one more time, go down to the kitchen and do your work.

DINA But— but—

CECILIE Do you hear me?

DINA I hear you and I obey. *(curtsies and exits to the left)*

Scene 2: CECILIE, BRUN

BRUN *(entering)* Good morning my dear Cecilie. How are you?

CECILIE You know very well, Father.

BRUN Yes, yes, I know, but you seem to me to be somewhat unreasonable. You have to expect that the abrupt change in lifestyle is somewhat unpleasant in the beginning. We've only been here six months and aren't completely familiar with the way things are done here. But it will come. Business isn't as good as we would wish, but it looks like it will go better than in the old country. You know as well as I how that ended up.

CECILIE Yes, it all went wrong, and it seems to me that that will happen here, too.

BRUN Yes, yes, I can't say that business is brilliant, but we can't expect everything at once either. When we have been here a few years and—

CECILIE No, Father, I will never be able to stay here and neither do I expect to find the kind of circumstances we had at home. It is intolerable here. Just consider the servant girl—she is so impudent and brazen. So— so— so intolerable that I am tempted to box her ears.

BRUN That is true enough, she is quite impudent. But my dear Cecilie, you must treat her as kindly as possible or else she may pack her things and leave, just as the others have done. In the three months we've been here we have tried a dozen different girls and all were worse than Dina. She is impudent, that is true, but at least she doesn't steal like several of the others did, and she pays attention to her work as well.

CECILIE She pays attention to her work! Yes, I can see it now. You don't know the half of what she does wrong. Don't think that I'm telling you everything, I know you have more than enough to think about.

Scene 3: BRUN, CECILIE, DINA

DINA *(comes running in)* Miss Cecilie! Miss Cecilie! Hurry down to the kitchen! The roast is burning up.

CECILIE No, for heaven's sake, Dina! Now you have gone too far! *(exits)*

BRUN Why don't you go down and help her?

DINA That isn't necessary. Miss Cecilie can manage on her own.

BRUN *(feeling his pockets)* Where is my wallet? What have I done with it?

DINA It's right here on the piano. You put it there an hour ago. *(hands him the wallet)*

BRUN *(takes the wallet) (aside)* My God. How careless of me! All my money! I am lucky that Dina is such an honest girl.

DINA *(grabs the wallet from him)* Why here is a pile of money, Mr. Brun, and still Miss Cecilie does nothing but complain. And *you*, Father! *(shaking her finger at Brun) You* complain, too! Oh, you are a rogue, Mr. Brun, you have much more money than you want people to think.

BRUN *(sits at the table counting the money)*

DINA *(singing, she looks in the mirror)*

BRUN Be quiet, Dina, you're disturbing me.

DINA *(dusts the piano and plays a little with one finger)*

BRUN Don't touch the piano, Dina. Leave it alone.

DINA I can't help it, Mr. Brun. My fingers begin to itch when I get near a piano.

BRUN When you don't know how to play, you should leave the piano alone.

DINA Can't play, you say? How do you know that I can't play?

BRUN Oh, a servant girl would never have the chance to learn it.

DINA Oh, is that so? Well, in that you are wrong. I have served in the homes of the rich for four years now and everyone had pianos in the house. I have had plenty of opportunity to learn to play.

BRUN But you haven't had any lessons?

DINA Oh yes, I have also had lessons. I've had a dozen boyfriends in my life, and among them were two musicians from whom I have learned music.

BRUN Ha, ha, ha, ha. It must have been delightful music that you learned from them!

DINA And so? You should have heard them play. One played a clarinet and the other a trumpet. So you could hear him from far away.

BRUN Ha, ha, ha, ha. So, you learned to play a trumpet?

DINA *(hits him)* I ask you not to insult him. He did not teach me to play a trumpet, but to play the piano—he could do that too.

BRUN Oh, right! How could that be? As long as a person is a servant there is no time to practice and without long and constant practice, there is no chance to learn.

DINA No time to practice, you say? Didn't I tell you that I have served in the homes of rich people where there were pianos in the house?

BRUN Did you really get permission to sit and play the piano?

DINA Get permission? Ha, ha, ha, ha. I gave myself permission, naturally.

BRUN And maybe in this house you also give yourself permission?

DINA Yes, naturally.

Brun I have never noticed it.

DINA Oh, I haven't been here more than a week yet. Just wait until I am a little more familiar with you and Miss Cecilie.

BRUN *(to himself)* Hmmm? I thought she was familiar enough the first day she came here. That was edifying to listen to.

DINA You don't think that I can play the piano, do you?

BRUN Naturally. If you say so, I have to believe it.

DINA So, you do believe that everything I said is true?

BRUN I assume that I have to believe it.

DINA Then, you don't think that I usually lie?

BRUN No, I don't think that.

DINA Do you really think well of me?

BRUN Yes, why not?

DINA You are the first person who has actually thought well of me and for that you shall have a kiss. *(she kisses him quickly)*

BRUN *(jumping from his chair, startled)* But— but— but, Dina! What is the meaning of this? This is going too far. You have to show some respect for the man of the house. I hope that is the first and last time that you take such liberties with me. *(seats himself again)*

DINA Nonsense. Don't pretend to be so righteous, Mr. Brun. You can't tell me that you are afraid of a kiss from a pretty young girl, for I know very well that I am pretty. All of my boyfriends have told me so many times; and I know that a man, even if he is sixty years old, likes to get a kiss from a pretty girl. So, you do not have to act as though you are angry about a kiss, that is pure hypocrisy. *(she looks at herself in the mirror)*

BRUN *(to himself)* She is right. *(aloud)* But Dina, it is *inappropriate*, and I tell you in all seriousness that in the future you must not take such liberties, and that— that— that—

DINA That, that, that? What "that"?

BRUN That— that— way! You do understand that there *must* be a difference between a master and a servant?

DINA Naturally there must be some difference, but not *too big* a difference. We are in a free country, you know.

BRUN *(interrupts)* But I tell you, I *do not* like it.

DINA Yes you *do*. Do you want one more? *(kisses him again quickly)*

BRUN *(stands up)* Dina, this is going too far. I— I— I—

DINA Brrrrrrr. Don't be so frightened. You need to stick your finger in the soil and smell what country you are in. We are here in a free country and here nothing is as it was back home. Just listen:

(quick speech with orchestral background, like a recitative)

Verse 1
Here in America things are not done as they are back home.
Here a girl can do as she pleases; she can even vote.
And if the mistress of the house wrinkles her nose,
what does that matter to the servant girl,

who simply packs her things
in her carpetbag and says,
"Many thanks, my dear Madam,"
for we are in a free country, you know,
in a free, free, free country, you know.

Verse 2
And if the mistress of the house is in a mood,
and should find it necessary to scold a servant girl,
then the girl is not afraid of slamming the door
and telling the mistress to kindly keep still.
And if the mistress then shouts, "No,
I won't accept this,"
the end, nevertheless, requires that she accept what is,
otherwise the servant girl neatly packs her things
in her carpetbag and says,
"Many thanks, my dear Madam,"
for we are in a free country, you know,
in a free, free, free country, you know.

Verse 3
And, should there be a fine piano in the house
and the servant girl wants to learn to play,
then she is to be welcomed as though in her own house,
and not as if she were just a visitor.
If the mistress of the house does not like it, she is to keep quiet,
and should the mistress come with the slightest protest,
immediately the servant girl bows and
neatly packs her things
in her carpetbag and says,
"Many thanks, my dear Madam,"
for we are in a free country, you know,
in a free, free, free country, you know.

Verse 4
And should the servant girl go on a visit and not have fine gloves
to wear,
she needn't ask what is yours or mine—she need not research
matters of ownership,

she simply takes the mistress's gloves and if the mistress says
she must not,
she neatly packs her things
in her carpetbag and says,
"Many thanks, my dear Madam,"
for we are in a free country, you know,
in a free, free, free country, you know.

(during the conclusion of Dina's recitation, Cecilie enters, clasps her hands together and stands there observing the scene)

DINA Now, I must go down to the kitchen and look after the roast, but first I want to show you that I can play. *(runs to the piano and plays a short, lively tune)* You see, I can play. *(runs out)*

Scene 4: BRUN, CECILIE

CECILIE You know, Father, this has gone too far.

BRUN *(restless)* Yes, yes, too far.

CECILIE Then how can you allow her to sit there and play?

BRUN Allow? I have not allowed her to play.

CECILIE Well, how can you put up with it then?

BRUN Yes, put up with it, what else can I do?

CECILIE Well, something must be done. This cannot continue.

BRUN That's true enough, but what?

CECILIE What?

BRUN Yes, what? I don't know what we can do.

CECILIE Well, I do, I am going to teach her a lesson.

BRUN A lesson? You tried that with the other servant girls we had, but what was the result? You no sooner started your "lessons" than the maid packed her things with a thank you very much.

CECILIE But Dina won't.

BRUN Why not?

CECILIE Because she is— is— is—

BRUN A little better than the other maids we have had? But that cannot be a reason to treat her in a way that causes her to leave us.

CECILIE Then let us try to make do without a servant girl.

BRUN Oh, we've tried that too. Haven't we agreed that things were worse for us without a servant? You can't stand to wash and scrub or iron or cook.

CECILIE Well, whatever happens, happens. I can no longer tolerate a servant girl who plays the piano right under our very noses.

BRUN Oh, I think you will find that there will be more that you have to tolerate. Just wait until Dina begins to feel more familiar in the house.

CECILIE More familiar? Is she not already familiar enough?

BRUN Yes, in my opinion, but not in her own opinion.

CECILIE My dear father, let's return to Norway.

BRUN And again find ourselves unable to make a living?

CECILIE Oh, I saw that people survived there too.

BRUN Naturally, but when someone back home finds themselves on their knees, it is difficult to get up again. Here, on the other hand, there are many possibilities. If one way doesn't work, there is another. As a result, it would be remarkable not to get a good position. Let us be patient for a couple years, then you will see that it will be all right, as they say.

Scene 5: BRUN, CECILIE, DINA

DINA *(rushes in)* Dinner is ready. The roast is a little burned, but I hope that it will be better tomorrow.

CECILIE Yes, and I hope that from now on you pay better attention to your work.

DINA Tomorrow we will both pay better attention, Miss.

BRUN *(to Cecilie)* Come on, Cecilie, let's go and eat. *(goes out with Cecilie)*

Scene 6: DINA, alone

DINA *(looking in mirror, admiring herself)* Oh my God, what fun it would be to be a fine lady with nothing to do but scolding the servant girl and putting on airs. Why couldn't I be a fine lady? I know I am attractive enough. It's not often one meets a fine lady as attractive as I am. I have nice skin, too— but *(looking at her hands)* my hands are too big and the skin too rough. Maybe it would help to rub in lard or some other kind of fat, I will try. No, that doesn't matter, because fine ladies wear gloves anyway. *(she picks up a pair of gloves lying on the piano and admires them)* Oh, they look beautiful. *(she picks up a bottle of eau de cologne and sprays herself with it)* Ahh, it smells wonderful!— but this dumb glove won't go on my hand. *(she pulls hard on the glove)* Oops, it split, darn— oh it doesn't matter, but the other one fits nicely. I wonder what it's like to play with gloves on? *(plays)*

Scene 7: DINA, CECILIE

CECILIE *(enters)* No, Dina, no one can eat that roast, it is completely spoiled. This is unforgivable carelessness. But— but— my God! What are you doing to my gloves?

DINA Oh, I'm just trying them on, to see how they fit.

CECILIE I fail to understand how it can be of any interest to you whether they fit or not when the gloves do not belong to you.

DINA I just wanted to see what my hands would look like with gloves on. See here! Don't you think they look good?

CECILIE If you want gloves, buy your own and let me keep mine for my own use. You will stretch them completely. How can you be so presumptuous with my things?

DINA We are in a free country, you know.

CECILIE Free country and free country. Heaven save us from your freedom which consists of impudence.

DINA Why are you making such a fuss just because I tried your gloves on?

CECILIE Fuss? How can you presume to talk to me that way?

DINA *(angry, snaps her fingers and exits to the left)*

CECILIE *(alone)* My God! What a country! and what people! Today she tries on my gloves, tomorrow she uses them. On the day after that she will try on my new dress and the day after that, she will wear it. Before long, she will have tried and used all my things and I will no longer be able to use them. I'm going to put a stop to this scandalous behavior in good time. I will seriously forbid her to do it.

DINA *(enters wearing a shawl and hat, with a carpetbag in her hand)* Miss Cecilie! I have the honor of saying good-bye. You can use the salary I am due for this week's work to buy yourself a pair of new gloves. *(with a proud, comical expression)* Farewell! Kiss your father for me! Farewell!

CECILIE *(restless)* Dina! Dina, do you hear me?

DINA Do you wish to speak with me?

CECILIE Where are you going?

DINA You know very well, I am leaving to look for another position, where people aren't so picky about a glove more or less.

CECILIE Listen here, Dina. Of all the servant girls we have had in the time we have been here, you are the only one we can say with certainty that she does not steal.

DINA *(bowing)* I am especially grateful for the compliment. So?

CECILIE And since you have such a strong sense of honor, I hope you will do the right thing.

DINA I hope so too.

CECILIE Well, then tell me, do you think it was right to burn the roast so that we could not eat it?

DINA No, of course not.

CECILIE But, why did you do it then?

DINA I didn't burn the roast.

CECILIE Who did, then?

DINA The fire, you know. *(turning away)*

CECILIE Stop fooling around and be serious, was it right to burn the roast?

DINA No, it wasn't.

CECILIE I knew it, and I know you will be honest and admit your mistake regarding the gloves. Do you think it was right of you to force my small gloves on your large hands? You know your hands are much larger than mine?

DINA Is that a question?

CECILIE No, it is not a question. *(shows her hands)* You can plainly see that my hands are much smaller.

DINA Let's measure. *(measuring)* Well, they are the same.

CECILIE So you admit that my gloves are too small for your hands?

DINA Oh yes.

CECILIE So do you also admit that you were wrong?

DINA Well, we have now arrived at the heart of the matter in our conflict. You say that it was wrong of me to try your small gloves on my big hands.

CECILIE Of course.

DINA But, do you remember that a couple of days ago, when it was raining and the street was muddy, and you had a quick errand right across the street, that you took my small shoes on your big feet. Did you not do that?

CECILIE Yes, I did, but what did that hurt?

DINA Well, I hope you are honest enough to admit that your feet are much bigger than mine. Just look at my delicate little foot *(shows her foot)* while yours is big and plump. *(pulls up Cecilie's dress slightly in front)*

CECILIE *(slaps at Dina's hand)* No, Dina, you are too crude. Uff! These American servant girls are unbearable trolls!

DINA Am I also a troll?

CECILIE You are just like all the others, a shameless, impudent girl.

DINA Miss, *(with a contemptuous curtsy)* I have the honor to take my leave—farewell!

Scene 8/9: DINA, CECILIE, BRUN*

BRUN *(enters from the right)* What is it? Where are you going, Dina?

DINA Farewell, Mr. Brun! *(shakes his hand firmly)* Thank you for the time we have had together. I am no longer needed in the house.

BRUN But— but— What is it then? What is it?

CECILIE She had the audacity to put my small gloves on her big hands and tear them.

DINA And the other day she put my small shoes on her big feet and now she is upset because I proved that her feet were bigger than mine. *(lifts Cecilie's dress)* You can see, Mr. Brun, that her feet are much bigger than mine. *(speaks more quickly and louder to keep Cecilie from contradicting her)* See what a delicate little foot I have, *(shows her foot)* so there can be no question about which of us is most ladylike. Everybody says that in order to be a fine lady, one must have small feet. *(speaks faster and louder)* Of course, she does have smaller hands than me, but she has bigger feet and I figure that my small feet measure up against her small hands and she has no reason to be stuck-up *(speaks even faster)* and so maybe I am just as fine as she is and maybe the time will come when I am a fine and rich lady—for we are in a free country, you know. And maybe also the day will come when Miss Cecilie will have to take a position as a servant girl, and maybe she will serve in my house. *(Brun and Cecilie both try unsuccessfully to speak)* No, wait! I'm not finished yet. As I said, it isn't impossible that I can become a fine and elegant lady. I have a pretty face and I can play the piano and— everything. So there is no need to be stuck-up, because the truth be told—

BRUN My dear Dina. Allow me to speak for a second.

DINA Dear me! Mr. Brun has the floor.

*Thrane wrote a second version of Scene 8 as Scene 9. Except for the last part of the scene, the action and the dialogue are similar. The second version (given here) is clearly the better dialogue and is therefore Scene 8/9.

BRUN I am going to allow myself to make a suggestion.

DINA All right, let's hear it.

BRUN Can we have a truce on one condition, that I give you one dollar more a week in return for which you will be more— more— more... not so— not so— so... well, I think you know what I mean.

DINA Yes, I understand, but there can never be a truce on those conditions, for we are in a free country, you know. When you want to give me one dollar more per week in order that I be "not so— not so—," then I assume you mean not so impudent. But impudent, what is that? Impudence is just a concept that does not exist here in America and when we are in America, then we are in America, right?

BRUN *(bewildered)* Wha— What?

DINA I said: When we are in America, then we are in America, right?

BRUN Naturally!

DINA And when we are in America, we have to be American. Habits and customs in the new world are not like habits and customs in the old world. Here there is freedom and equality, for we are in a free country, you know, and when we are in a free country, then it isn't proper to be so hoity-toity and put on such stately airs. Domestics have a rule that we are to be independent and self-reliant, and you must understand that in a free country, a servant must be just as free as the master—otherwise this wouldn't be a free country.

BRUN I— I— I beg your pardon?

DINA A servant girl must have the freedom to be treated nicely and when she is not treated nicely, she packs her things in her travel bags and says, "Many thanks."

BRUN *(repeats in same tone)* Many thanks.

DINA Oh, no need to thank me. I hope that you now understand what I mean, so I don't need to say more.

BRUN Oh, no. It is perfectly clear.

DINA Well? What impression do you have of what I said?

BRUN Impression? Impression?

DINA Yes, impression, yes, or maybe it has not made an impression?

BRUN Oh yes, God knows I have gotten an impression, a significant impression.

DINA What impression then?

BRUN Well, your little speech has given me the impression that there are significant difficulties in the way of a truce.

DINA All right, then I have the honor of taking my leave. *(takes her bag and begins to go)* Farewell! *(kisses Brun's hand)*

BRUN No, no, no. Wait. There may be some difficulties, but I did not say that the difficulties could not be surmounted. I think we can find a way out of this. Listen, my dear Dina, you like white gloves, do you not?

DINA Naturally.

BRUN Well, here is two dollars to buy yourself a pair.

DINA *(kisses him quickly)* Thank you, Mr. Brun. You are a gentleman.

BRUN *(takes a handkerchief and dries his mouth)* But— my—

CECILIE *(enters as Dina is kissing Brun, slaps her hands together)* No, this is going too far!

Scene 10: BRUN, DINA, CECILIE, POSTMAN

POSTMAN *(enters from the background carrying two letters)* Mr. Brown! *(leaves)*

BRUN *(opens first letter)* Hmmmm, business. *(opens the second letter)* It's from old Petersen!

CECILIE Really? How nice.

BRUN *(as he reads, Cecilie moves to his left side and reads along, while Dina moves close to his right side and also reads along)* Well, that is nice. Petersen's son is going to make a tour of America and wants to visit Chicago.

CECILIE Young Petersen coming here? But what's he going to do here?

BRUN Business.

CECILIE What else does it say?

BRUN Ahh... nothing, really.

DINA *(grabs the letter)* Oh yes there is, Miss Cecilie, there is much more. *(holds the letter with her left hand while using her right hand to keep Brun away)* It says... that the young Petersen is a promising young man and his father would not mind it if a connection could be established—hurrah! You are getting a sweetheart, Miss Cecilie. Yes, and it's about time. Oh, you can believe that it is fun to have a sweetheart, I've had a dozen sweethearts, so I speak from experience.

BRUN *(takes back the letter) (ironically)* Can I have the floor for a moment?

DINA *(with a comical expression and her hands behind her back)* Mr. Brun has the floor.

BRUN I have something to talk to Cecilie about, so I would appreciate it if you left us alone for a moment.

DINA Naturally, I am not nosy. I have enough to do down in the kitchen. *(she exits)*

Scene 11: BRUN, CECILIE

CECILIE Oh, my God! That girl!

BRUN Yes, she is presumptuous, but what are we to do?

CECILIE What else is in the letter?

BRUN Well, you've got the wrong impression. I cannot deny that I am pleasantly surprised because, not only will I be able to get out of my financial difficulties, but *(holds Cecilie under her chin)* my dear Cecilie! I also hope there can be a small change in this for you. Young Petersen is an attractive young man, a good businessman and all. Who knows? You might even come to like him.

CECILIE *(feigning bashfulness)* Oh, don't talk about such things.

BRUN No, no, but we can always perhaps talk about it. You see, old man Petersen makes it very clear that he wouldn't mind a relationship between you and his son, and it would make a good match for you too, my dear Cecilie. What do you think?

CECILIE Well, if that is your opinion, then—

BRUN So, then it is your opinion too. Yes, that is the right decision my dear Cecilie. *(claps his hands)* You are a reasonable girl. But when he comes now, you must not be too withdrawn, you know. Men like that can be so bashful around women.

CECILIE *(interrupting)* Yes, I understand, but *(looking around)* a rich man's son surely expects to be welcomed in a more elegant house than this...

BRUN *(looking around)* Y...e...s! Perhaps so!

CECILIE This is unacceptable. It looks too poor here, and you know that first impressions can be decisive.

BRUN Yes, maybe so, but what can we do?

CECILIE First and foremost, we have to buy carpets, and then we need new curtains—

BRUN Carpets? But that is too expensive.

CECILIE We *must*—and we also need a new tea service.

BRUN Yes, ahh, that's true, but—

CECILIE And I must have a new dress.

BRUN Yes, I suppose so.

CECILIE And when can we expect him?

BRUN According to the letter, we can expect him any day now.

CECILIE So there is no time to waste. We must go shopping immediately.

BRUN Yes, you're right. Get ready and we will go.

CECILIE *(exits left and returns wearing a hat and shawl)*

BRUN *(to himself)* Yes, would that they become a couple—Cecilie and the young Petersen.

CECILIE I'm ready, Father! Here is your hat! *(they exit)*

Scene 12: DINA, alone

DINA *(enters)* Finally. For the first time, I am finally alone in the house.

What shall I begin with? Yes, first, a little music. *(sits at the piano and plays) (after playing a while, she goes over to the mirror where she makes several gestures and practices poses for polite behavior)* I can be a fine lady. There is nothing wrong with that. I wonder how I would look in a new scarf and white gloves. And imagine a Grecian band bracelet... *(snaps her fingers)* That I'd like to see. I think I'll go into Miss Cecilie's room and try on her newest dresses. *(goes)*

Scene 13: PETERSEN, alone

PETERSEN *(enters from the background, elegantly dressed)* So, I have finally reached the goal of my journey. Here is the house of my future wife. Curious that I haven't seen her! I don't know her, but more importantly, my father has told me so much about her. And, according to her picture, at least I know that she is pretty! Now the questions is, will she have me. We'll have to wait and see. But there is no one home. Well, I suppose one must be patient. Patience wins out in the end. *(looks in a book that is lying on the piano)* Ah, a novel. So, she is romantic! I cannot deny that my heart beats a little quicker. One never knows how one will be welcomed. *(pause)* But there is no one in the house? *(coughs loudly)* Somebody should come soon. *(pause)* What a nice guitar. That proves she is a perfect lady— Ah! There is a pair of gloves, she must have beautiful small hands. *(pause)* Hm! Hm! No one here. *(goes to the back door and coughs)*

Scene 14: PETERSEN, DINA

DINA *(enters, elegantly dressed)* La, la, la, la, la. *(dances without seeing Petersen who is standing by the back door)* Now I am a perfect lady. *(looks at herself in the mirror)* It feels wonderful to be in an outfit like this. I wish I could go to the theater in this dress, or to a ball. Oh, yes, I can see myself dancing the quadrille. *(dances the quadrille, reaching her right hand to her imaginary partner)*

PETERSEN *(grabs her outstretched hand)*

DINA *(startled, she screams and wants to run offstage to the left)*

PETERSEN *(holding her back)* You must excuse me for interrupting you in your dance.

DINA Oh! Oh!

PETERSEN *(to himself)* How lovely she is! She is even prettier than her photograph! What eyes! *(to Dina)* Excuse me, Miss Cecilie.

DINA *(to herself)* He thinks I'm Miss Cecilie. What fun!

PETERSEN The portrait you sent home to us is just like you, Miss Cecilie, but it also isn't exactly like you. You are much prettier in person.

DINA The portrait looks like me, you say?

PETERSEN Considerably so.

DINA *(to herself)* He has a powerful imagination!

PETERSEN You know, your father and my father were childhood friends.

DINA Yes, we received your father's letter just today wherein he informed us that we could expect you, but we didn't expect you so soon.

PETERSEN Perhaps I came too early?

DINA A dear guest never comes too early.

PETERSEN *(kisses her hand)* Thank you for saying that, Miss Cecilie.

DINA Please, have a seat. *(they sit down)*

PETERSEN Well, eh— I have had a quick trip.

DINA Really?

PETERSEN And quite nice weather.

DINA Hm, hm!

PETERSEN I stayed in New York for a couple of days, then took a train directly to Chicago.

DINA I see.

PETERSEN Hm, are you not well, Miss Cecilie?

DINA Me? Oh, yes! I'm as healthy as a horse. *(to herself)* For God's sake, I better talk a little more. If one is to be a fine lady, the mouth will have to grind like a peppermill. *(to Petersen)* Oh no, far from it. I am not sick— well, for the time being I do feel a bit of a pressure in my chest, *(releases a deep sigh)* but generally, I am quite healthy. How about you, are you sick?

PETERSEN Oh no, far from it.

DINA What do you think of Chicago?

PETERSEN Oh, I just got here this moment, and don't really have any opinion about the place, but on the other hand, any place where you lived would be wonderful.

DINA Really, what fun.

PETERSEN *(to himself)* She is really naive.

DINA *(to herself)* What can I find to talk about? Hm. The weather is wonderful today.

PETERSEN Very nice.

DINA But tomorrow, it will be even nicer.

PETERSEN Really? How do you know that?

DINA Oh, that much is easy to predict.

PETERSEN Predict? Ha, ha, ha. Perhaps you tinker a little with the art of fortune-telling?

DINA Oh, maybe.

PETERSEN No, really? Then you must tell my fortune. *(stretches out his hand)*

DINA *(takes his hand and looks at it)* I can see— here I can see— *(to herself)* What can I say? *(aloud)* This line means marriage— yes— it is quite obvious.

PETERSEN What is obvious?

DINA That you are soon to be married.

PETERSEN *(to himself)* How naive can one be? *(aloud)* But you, Miss Cecilie, *(takes her hand)* don't you see anything in your own hand?

DINA Yes, I too will soon be married.

PETERSEN *(to himself)* No, she is exceptionally naive. *(aloud)* Do you have more to tell me?

DINA Oh, yes. I have a great deal to tell you: America is a magnificent country; you have never seen such a country; it's as big as all of the Scandinavian countries put together, and everything you can think of grows here. It's good for you—that you came here. I am so happy that you came over here. You will be very happy in America, and especially here in Chicago. *(looks into his hand)* Yes, you will be very happy.

PETERSEN *(to himself)* Her naiveté has no boundary!

DINA *(still looking into his hand)* This line here shows the heart wandering down the path of love, and this line alongside the other means love in return, and these small, fine lines stand for many little—

PETERSEN *(to himself)* What heavenly innocence! A more innocent girl would be impossible to find. Oh, how I already love her!

DINA *(releasing his hand)* Now I am not able to tell you anything more.

PETERSEN You have said everything I had hoped to know. Tell me, Miss Cecilie, may I presume that you speak French?

DINA Certainly.

PETERSEN *Avez vous été dans la belle France?*

DINA *Oui, Monsieur.*

PETERSEN *Et vous aimez la France?*

DINA *Oui, Monsieur.*

PETERSEN *Et vous jouez au piano?*

DINA *Oui, Monsieur.*

PETERSEN Do you also sing?

DINA Naturally.

PETERSEN Oh, perhaps you would sing a song for me?

DINA Yes, as many as you might wish.

PETERSEN Thank you.

DINA No problem. *(plays and sings a piece)*

PETERSEN That was a pretty song.

DINA So, you liked it?

PETERSEN Remarkable! Have you studied music long?

DINA Oh yes, since I was as little as— But, please, won't you sit down?

PETERSEN Thank you.

DINA No problem.

(pause)

PETERSEN I— it was— Hm. Hm.

(pause)

DINA *(to herself)* What is there to talk about?

PETERSEN You see— Miss Cecilie? As I said, from the moment I first saw your photograph, you have made a deep impression on me. But now that I have seen the original, I cannot find the right words to express my admiration for you. Precious Cecilie, our parents have determined that we belong together. Fate—Providence itself—has determined that we belong together. I love you until death. Your being, your innocence, your naiveté, your talents: all are formed to make a man happy. Oh, Cecilie! Let me be that lucky man! I feel that I cannot live without you!

DINA *(to herself)* What the hell do I do now? Now I am really in a bind. What will Miss Cecilie say if I steal her sweetheart?

PETERSEN Answer me, Cecilie, please answer me. Will you be mine?

DINA *(to herself)* Steal Miss Cecilie's sweetheart? We all have a little larceny in our soul. One has to be a little smart if one is to amount to anything here in America.

PETERSEN Answer me, Miss Cecilie. Don't torture me any longer.

DINA Never mind. *(throws herself into his arms)*

PETERSEN Oh, what joy! My childhood dreams are fulfilled. *(takes both her hands and looks into her eyes)* So, you are mine. Cecilie, do you promise to love me forever?

DINA Yes, of course! *(scratches herself behind her ear) (to herself)* But what am I to do? They are expected back any moment— then what? Well, having said A, one must also say B. The comedy must be played out. Here, I forced myself to become a wife and he is duty bound to stand by his word! Yes, I'll take him. Such opportunities don't come every day.

PETERSEN Why are you so quiet, my love? What are you thinking about?

DINA Well, you can perfectly well understand that in a time such as this, it is natural that one think of the seriousness of the moment.

PETERSEN True enough. But in this moment, I should like to see you cheerful and happy, just as I am. Oh, you don't know how happy I feel.

DINA *(to herself)* But what am I to do? We must get out of here before they return. *(aloud)* Listen, my friend, what is your name?

PETERSEN My name is Fredrik.

DINA Fredrik? Oh, yes, that's right. But now listen, my dear Fredrik, what are we going to do?

PETERSEN Do? I suppose we have nothing else to do but to love each other.

DINA True enough, but— my father— he—

PETERSEN Yes, that's true. We must first have your father's permission.

DINA Oh no, that isn't necessary. My father gave his permission long ago.

PETERSEN Well, then that is no problem. All you have to do is introduce me to your father.

DINA But, that cannot be done.

PETERSEN Why not?

DINA Because my father has left for New Orleans on business and he will be gone all winter.

PETERSEN You mean, you are home alone?

DINA Yes, of course.

PETERSEN Well then, let's go down to New Orleans to your father.

DINA Yes, I think that's my view too, but—

PETERSEN Let's leave today, this moment.

DINA But, we can't travel such a long distance together without— without— *(bites her fingers)*

PETERSEN What do you mean?

DINA I mean: it wouldn't be proper that we travel such a long distance together without being married.

PETERSEN Well then, let's get married before we travel.

DINA Yes, you know how people like to have something to talk about.

PETERSEN Yes, you are absolutely right. We have to marry immediately, and then travel.

DINA *(runs offstage to the left and returns wearing Cecilie's hat and coat)*

PETERSEN *(while Dina is out)* I guess that is what you call getting married in a hurry. Well, it is the American way. Back home, such things could never happen.

DINA I'm ready.

PETERSEN *(offers her his arm)* Me too. Is it far to a notary public?

DINA No, we can find a justice of the peace nearby. *(they go to the back door)*

DINA *(opens the door carefully, jumps back in alarm, pulls Petersen aside) (to herself)* How annoying that he should show up this very minute.

PETERSEN What is it? What is it?

DINA It's— it's— it's a disgusting person who comes here regularly once a week— in order to— well, he did me a little favor once, and so—

PETERSEN I understand.

DINA *(to herself)* What do I tell him? *(aloud)* Dear Fredrik, do me a favor and go into that room over there for a moment. *(she points to the left, and taps him on his cheek)*

PETERSEN As you wish, my love. *(he exits)*

Scene 15: DINA, MILLER

MILLER *(enters with an instrument in his hand, slightly drunk, singing)*

Whoever has not been drunk
is truly not a man.
Whoever only moderately slakes his thirst
had better not begin.

Then everything goes round and round
in our Capitalum.* Whoever has not been drunk... *(etc.)*

DINA Quiet! Stop making such a racket!

MILLER *(puts his arm around her waist and pats her shoulder)* How are you, *mein allerliebste* Dina. Now you shall be mine and I shall be yours. *(sings)*
Give me your hand, my darling,
come to my castle with me.
Come, we'll be together forever.
It is not far from here...

DINA *(in the meantime, she has torn herself loose, stamps her feet, and says aside)* Damn Dutchman!

MILLER How beautiful you are, Dina. You are prettier now than you have ever been. *(sings)*
You have— you have diamonds and pearls,
you have the most beautiful eyes...

(puts his arm around her, tries to kiss her)

DINA *(sulking)* Leave me alone.

MILLER *(hands at his side)* Well, well, how stingy the maiden has become.

DINA It seems that you do not consider me a lady.

MILLER *Lady*? The devil you say! Have you become a lady now? Then you are probably not a maiden anymore either?

DINA *(slaps him on the mouth)*

MILLER Ouch, ouch! I humbly beg your pardon, it was not as ill meant as it was said. No, I mean that it was not as ill thought as it was said. *(embraces her again)*

DINA *(cuffs him on the ear)*

MILLER What was that for?

DINA That will teach you to think everything of me.

---

*Thrane's Latin is uncertain here. He probably means *capitulum*, a diminutive of *caput*, meaning "little head."

MILLER Naturally I think only everything good about you.

DINA What do you want? Why did you come here?

MILLER What do I want? That was one hell of a question! *(takes a letter out of his pocket)* Here in this letter have you yourself written that I should come as soon as possible so that we could get married. And here you write that you will get rid of all your other boyfriends and hereafter keep yourself true to me alone, and so I came all the way from St. Louis and now you ask me what I am doing here? Are you crazy, Dina?

DINA Are you crazy, you Dutchman?

MILLER My love, my heart, my treasure!

DINA Leave me alone, I say. Get out of here—there will never be a marriage between us—I don't want any Dutchman.

MILLER What? Are you chasing me away once again? No, no, no, my pretty! We'll have none of that. You've made a fool of me again and again, but this time, you will not make a fool of me.

DINA *(snaps the letter out of his hands and tears it in two)* Get out of here. I don't want to see you anymore. I am an American, you know. I don't want any lager beer.

MILLER No, I'm not going. I'm staying and you are to come, this minute, with me to the courthouse so we can get married.

DINA No, siree! I will not marry you. I can make a much better match.

MILLER Listen, Dina! Don't make me angry. You will marry me, and right now. If not, I will— *(shouts and stamps his foot)*

DINA *(looking around)* Hush! Hush! Don't make such a racket!

MILLER And if you do not marry me now, then— *(hits the table violently)*

DINA Hush, hush. *(looking anxiously around)* Yes, yes, I will marry you. Just be quiet, don't make a scene!

MILLER Will you marry me?

DINA Yes, of course I will. I will be your wife.

MILLER Well, let's go, now!

DINA Just let me put my nice silk dress on first.

MILLER Silk dress? What nonsense!

DINA Yes, when I stand at the altar, I want to be as pretty as possible in order to please my beloved Fritz. *(places her hand under his chin)*

MILLER *(pats her hand)* Ah, you are lovely!

DINA While I am out getting dressed, I want you to sit with your instrument and sing a song. Sing the one you know I like.

MILLER No! I don't feel like singing right now.

DINA *(tenderly)* Don't you want to sing when your darling little wife asks you to? Dear Fritz!

MILLER All right, I'll sing for you, as often as you want, and when you want! *(seats himself at the piano, plays a prelude, sings)*

DINA *(exits left. Returns holding Petersen's hand, walking on tiptoe, begins to sneak out the back door. Dina opens the door, jumps back, startled. She pulls Petersen with her out to the left again.)*

MILLER *(during the song, Miller sits with his back to Dina and Petersen. After the song begins, he starts to straighten his right trouser leg, humming a polka.)*

Scene 16: MILLER, BRUN, CECILIE

(Brun and Cecilie enter, see Miller and are surprised. They nod to each other, talk together, assuming that Miller is Petersen)

MILLER Tralala...la...la.

BRUN *(to Cecilie)* It is your young Petersen. He is just like his portrait.

CECILIE Yes, there can be no doubt.

BRUN *(taps Miller on the shoulder)* Welcome to Chicago, my young friend!

MILLER Oh! ah, thank you.

BRUN There is no need to ask who you are, my God, how you resemble your father. Welcome, welcome, my young friend! We hadn't expected you for a couple of days, but the sooner you came, the better.

MILLER Thank you very much. *(to himself)* What the devil is all this about?

BRUN Cecilie! Would you please get us some wine so we can toast him welcome?

CECILIE *(exits)*

BRUN *(to Miller)* Yes, yes, that's the way it goes. We live in a remarkable world. At the very least, I dreamed that my daughter— Yes, I said— I want to say: Your father and I were good friends when we were young.

CECILIE *(enters carrying a tray with three glasses and two carafes)*

BRUN Well, let's have a little glass of wine—what do you prefer to drink?

MILLER Whiskey, thank you!

CECILIE Whiskey!!!

BRUN Well, to each his own. There is no arguing taste— Cecilie! Bring in some Bourbon.

CECILIE *(exits)*

BRUN As I was saying, I and your father were good friends, classmates, you see.

CECILIE *(enters with the whiskey)*

BRUN Well, here is the whiskey, it's good old Bourbon. Cheers, Mr. Petersen!

MILLER *(to himself)* So, my name is Petersen. It's good to find that out. But God in heaven knows what Petersen I am supposed to be.

BRUN Well, my young friend. Let's sit and talk for a while. *(they are seated)* How long have you been traveling?

MILLER Thirty-six hours.

BRUN Thirty-six hours? Oh, you mean from New York. No, I mean from Norway.

MILLER Oh that. *(to himself)* Norway must be a hell of distance! *(aloud)* Oh, I guess it's about four months since I left Norway.

BRUN *Four* months, you say? God help us, were you shipwrecked along the way?

MILLER Shipwrecked? N...o— yes, yes! That's true, we were shipwrecked on the Madeira Islands.

BRUN On the Madeira Islands you say? Did you sail as far south as the Madeira Islands?

MILLER Well, you see, as a matter of fact we had to stop in Turkey.

BRUN In Turkey, you say? That was a remarkable voyage, how can this be?

MILLER Well, to be perfectly honest, Mr. Petersen—

BRUN Petersen?

MILLER Did I say Petersen?

BRUN Yes, yes, you were saying— you meant Brown, of course.

MILLER Yes, of course I meant that— it is me who is named Petersen, and you are called Brown. That is correct, isn't it?

CECILIE *(to herself)* This young man is very strange.

BRUN Yes, yes, you're probably somewhat confused after your long trip.

MILLER Yes, exactly. I am absolutely confused. Excuse me. One more glass should help to make me all right. *(drinks two glasses of whiskey)*

CECILIE Tell me, how is your sister, Lovise?

MILLER Oh, very well, thank you. You can believe she has become a fine young girl.

BRUN Girl, you say?

CECILIE But father, didn't you tell me that she had married?

MILLER Yes, yes, of course, she is married. No, I meant my younger sister.

CECILIE Do you have a younger sister? *(to Brun)* But father, why have you not told me about that?

BRUN Do you have a younger sister? That's remarkable, I thought—

MILLER Well, not sister, exactly—it is a young girl that father adopted and who I call my sister.

CECILIE Oh, is that it?

MILLER Yes, that's it.

BRUN Oh, there is one more thing. Tell me now, how is business for my old friend? How much did he export last year?

MILLER Oh, I guess about 10,000 bushels.

BRUN Bushels, you say? Does he no longer have the timber business?

MILLER Oh no, far from it. *(to himself)* Damn it, the timber trade isn't measured in bushels! *(aloud)* He hasn't quit the timber business, but he has entered the grain trade.

BRUN The grain trade?

MILLER Oh yes, it is a very profitable business.

BRUN But I didn't know that Norway exported grain.

MILLER *(to himself)* Damn! This isn't going to work. One dumb thing after another. *(aloud)* Well, Mr. Peter— Mr. Brown, I mean, I am very tired following my journey and I am totally disoriented.

CECILIE Dear father. Don't bother Mr. Petersen with any more questions. You should know that he is not in a position to discuss business.

BRUN No, you are right, my dear Cecilie. Well, Mr. Petersen, let's talk about something else, something even more important. You see, your father, in his last letter, told me in all confidence why he sent you here. For my part, I have nothing against the match, quite the contrary, the sooner it can be arranged, the better. Everything is ready to go as far as your father and I are concerned. All that remains is that you and Cecilie can agree. I have prepared Cecilie, so you don't need to fear rejection. I'll leave you two alone for a moment. So get right to the matter, it's just as well to get it over and done with. *(he leaves)*

Scene 17: CECILIE, MILLER

MILLER *(to himself)* This much I can understand. My name is Petersen and I am a son of my father, that my father lives in Norway, and that the daughter of this house has been chosen for me and her name is Cecilie. That much I know, but will it profit me to propose marriage, that I don't know.

CECILIE *(to herself)* He leaves me sitting here without saying a single word to me.

MILLER *(to himself)* She is a pretty girl; it is a nice house. Her father seems to be a man in business with a good position. Well, I sure think I will profit by it.

CECILIE *(to herself)* For God's sake, isn't he going to say a word to me?

MILLER Hm, hm. Nice weather we're having today?

CECILIE Y...e...s.

MILLER *(to himself)* Well, if I am going to propose, I better do it quickly before Dina returns and spoils the game. Full speed ahead. *(aloud)* Miss Cecilie, you are very beautiful, very beautiful!

CECILIE Hm. Hm.

MILLER I admire you.

CECILIE Hm. Hm.

MILLER *(to himself)* No, first I need to have a drink for a little courage. *(takes a glass of whiskey)* Miss Cecilie! What are you thinking about?

CECILIE Hm. Hm.

MILLER *(to himself)* Damn. She won't answer other than "hm," "hm." At this rate, we'll never reach the goal. I suspect that the only way to proceed is by direct attack. If I'm not mistaken, in the fancy world, it is customary to get down on one knee—all right—first a shot, then on my knees. *(takes another drink and throws himself on his knees)* Miss Cecilie!! You see me at your feet, I love you, will you be my wife?

CECILIE Hm! Hm!

MILLER You don't have to hesitate. It has long ago been decided that we would have each other. Can you answer?

CECILIE I...have...to...think...about...it.

MILLER No, no time to think about it. It's now or never. Just say the little word "yes," and everything will be all right.

CECILIE *(confused)* But, my God.

Scene 18: MILLER, CECILIE, PETERSEN, DINA, BRUN

BRUN *(he has been standing listening)* Now, Cecilie, don't stand on ceremony. Don't torture the young man. *(takes their hands and joins them)* You see, take each other, children, and be happy.

MILLER Thank you, Mr. Brown, thank you, noble father-in-law. How happy my father will be when he hears of our union.

BRUN I can see him now when he receives the letter telling him about it. He will immediately open a bottle of champagne—just between us, the old man enjoys a glass of wine.

MILLER But man needs wine, too.

BRUN Naturally, I am certainly no temperance man.

MILLER Don't you think we should celebrate the engagement with a toast?

BRUN Yes, of course. *(he pours)* So, children! Congratulations! May you live long and happy lives together— and that you— Yes, yes, the rest will come naturally. Now, cheers! *(all three drink)*

MILLER Thank you, Mr. Brown. As your son-in-law, I hope to make you happy and proud. *(flirts disgustingly with Cecilie as they touch glasses)*

BRUN *(pats him on the shoulder)* Don't worry, but listen. I don't care for beating around the bush or needless fussing, so let's get right down to matters. We have come this far, and we can just as well begin to talk about the wedding.

CECILIE But, Father—

BRUN You see, children, it is exactly twenty-six years ago today that I was married and it would be a special joy if you could have your wedding on the same day.

CECILIE But Father, you—

BRUN Isn't that true, Mr. Petersen?

MILLER Oh, yes, absolutely.

BRUN So *you* have nothing against having the wedding today?

MILLER Far from it. I am ready right now. How about you, Cecilie?

CECILIE This all comes so unexpectedly. I am not ready.

BRUN Nonsense. Mr. Petersen doesn't care what your dress is like and we will have no protestations. We will go to the justice of the peace and there take care of it in the American manner. Agreed?

MILLER That is just the way I wish it to be.

BRUN Well, Cecilie! Go into your room and get ready, but simply.

MILLER Simply.

CECILIE Very well, Father. Since you insist, I will do as you wish.

(Cecilie goes to the left, but recoils with a shriek. Brun and Miller rush to her. Dina and Petersen enter, Dina wearing Cecilie's dress)

BRUN Dina, in Cecilie's dress!

MILLER Dina, with a strange man!

DINA *(to herself)* Now, all depends on maintaining courage. *(aloud)* Honored ladies and gentlemen! I have the honor to introduce to you my future husband.

MILLER And I have the honor of introducing my future wife.

CECILIE *(takes Dina aside)* But Dina, What kind of comedy is this? Why are you wearing my dress, and who is this strange man?

DINA *(in English)* Mind your own business, Miss Cecilie!

BRUN *(to Petersen)* My good man, I cannot deny—

DINA *(to Petersen)* Come, Fredrik! Let us get out of here as quickly as possible—or we will be late for the train.

CECILIE No, just a minute, my dear mam'sell. I do not wish that you leave wearing my dress.

BRUN *(to Petersen)* My good man, I have nothing against you personally, but I must tell you directly that I do not want to see you again in my house in a room alone with my servant girl.

PETERSEN Your servant girl! What are you saying? What do you mean?

BRUN What do I mean? I mean just what I said. I am saying that it is totally inappropriate for you to go into a house and shut yourself in with the servant girl.

DINA *(to herself)* Here comes the explosion.

PETERSEN Of course, it would be most improper of me, but I think there must be a real misunderstanding here. You are speaking about your servant girl, you don't mean that lady over there? *(he points to Dina)*

BRUN Yes, I do.

PETERSEN Sir, I have not had the honor of making your acquaintance, but I am telling you that I will not accept any insult to my future wife. How dare you enter a strange house and insult the lady of the house?

BRUN A *strange* house, you say? Have you lost your senses? Don't you think I know where I live? *(turns)* This is *my* house, and this "lady," as you call her, is my servant girl, sir, and there is the door, sir. Do you understand me now?

PETERSEN May I kindly ask your name?

BRUN My name is Brown.

MILLER *(to himself)* Here it comes. Now a shot is really necessary!

PETERSEN And this lady *(points to Cecilie)* is your daughter Cecilie?

BRUN Yes, sir, and that young man *(points to Miller)* is Mr. Petersen, my future son-in-law.

MILLER At your service, glad to make your acquaintance, sir. *(offers his hand to Petersen)*

PETERSEN *(looks at Miller with disgust)* This is all beyond my understanding. This gentleman *(points to Miller)* is your future son-in-law, you say?

BRUN Yes, absolutely.

PETERSEN But I have traveled all the way from Norway to be your son-in-law.

MILLER *(hums)*

CECILIE *(throws herself on a chair)*

BRUN *(beside himself, confused)* But— but— but— how can this be? Who are you?

PETERSEN I am the son of Martin Petersen of Christiania.

DINA *(humming and drumming with her fingers)*

MILLER *(doing the same)*

BRUN *(confused)* *You*? You are the son of Martin Petersen?

PETERSEN That is what I told you.

BRUN Are you all trying to make fun of me? *(to Miller)* Then, who are you, my dear sir?

MILLER I am a man.

BRUN What is your name?

MILLER My name is Miller.

BRUN Miller? Miller, you say? Then how could you presume to call yourself Petersen?

MILLER I never have.

BRUN Have you never called yourself Petersen and won my daughter under false pretenses?

MILLER Far from it. I have not called myself Petersen, it is *you* who have called me Petersen. And I have not misrepresented myself to your daughter, you yourself offered her to me. Why should I not accept a precious gift from God when it drops right into my lap?

BRUN *(to himself)* Yes, he does have a point there. *(aloud)* But you, Dina, how could you presume to use my daughter's name and seduce our guest?

MILLER *(to Dina)* Now it's your turn to answer, Dina.

DINA I have not taken your daughter's name, *(speaks faster and faster)* but this fellow here had the pleasure to call me Cecilie and then declare his love for me and promise me marriage, and why should I not accept a gift from God when it drops into my lap? This fellow likes me and I like him and don't we have the right to marry each other without the permission of Mr. Brown and Miss Cecilie? *(curtsies sarcastically) (reaches for Petersen's arm)* Come, my dear Fredrik, let us go to city hall.

PETERSEN *(bows sarcastically)* Miss Dina! I am grateful for your tender feelings toward me, but you must...excuse me: I can no longer return them.

DINA So you want to break your promise of marriage? No, stop. I can understand you are a "greenhorn," but that is not done here in America, for we are in a free country, you know. You have promised marriage and if you do not keep your word, I will take you to court and then you will get a taste of American customs.

BRUN *(to Petersen)* Listen, my young friend. The only thing to do now is put a good face on a bad situation. If we can get out of this difficulty by offering a couple of thousand dollars, should we not do so? Anyway, think of the scandal!

PETERSEN You are right. Let us for God's sake avoid a scandal and the courts. I am willing to pay however many thousand are required.

BRUN My dear charming Dina! You are a good girl, right?

DINA *(in English)* That is a question?

BRUN You cannot have Mr. Petersen.

DINA *(in English)* Of course I can.

BRUN But you don't want to force a man to marry you?

DINA Of course I will.

BRUN Listen to reason; if you force Mr. Petersen to marry you, he will abandon you the next day. You will be left alone with no husband. Is it not best to get a husband one can keep?

DINA *(in English)* Certainly.

BRUN Well, I understand that that man there is a real sweetheart. If you go ahead and marry him, you won't have to worry about house or furniture. We will take care of it all. You will get a beautiful wedding present and if we should offer a couple of thousand dollars, there would be no objections.

DINA Well, a house and furniture are not necessary. I consider it more of an honor to have been offered. I only demand that Cecilie's and my wedding be held on the same day and here in this house.

BRUN That is all?

DINA And that in the future my husband and I will be considered friends in this house.

BRUN *(to himself)* I guess we'll have to swallow the bitter pill. *(aloud)* Naturally, my dear Dina. Miss Dina, *(introduces)* may I have the honor of introducing Mr. and Mrs. Miller! *(compliments all around)* Let us now send for a justice of the peace in order to join the loving couple and let us end the day in peace and joy. Mr. and Mrs. Miller! It will always be a pleasure to have you as guests in our house.

DINA *(turning to the audience)*

Now I ask if the audience found pleasure
in my presentation of the American girl?
What you think of the play is a matter for the author
but let me tell you that I demand applause
and if you don't clap wildly right now
you should know that I will be good and angry
and I will pack my things in my carpetbag and say,
"Many thanks, you will see me no more,"
for we are in a free country you know,
in a free, free, free country, you know.

THE CURTAIN FALLS

The Posting Station in Hallingdal

A NATIONAL MUSICAL IN TWO ACTS

Characters:

HALVOR RØKEN, posting station* proprietor

SNEFRID, his daughter

GUNHILD, girl from the farm

GURI, old woman

OLA, farmer and horse groom

ANDERS, cotter's son

LORD FITZGERALD, English tourist

A TRAVELER

PEER, posting station boy

Stage Properties:

Two rakes, 1 scythe, 1 whetstone, 1 clay pipe, 1 bandage wrap, 1 coffee cup, lumber, coins, woolen thread, three teeth, rifle, powder, lightning and thunder, 2 fish, 1 milk can, milk, coffee, a lur.**

Act 1

As the curtain goes up, Snefrid is alone in the background, standing on a mountain and playing a lur. To the right on the stage is a house. To the left is a barn and a forest.

Scene 1: SNEFRID

SONG NUMBER 1

SNEFRID

High in the mountains I roam with the animals,

*Posting stations were common in Norway until the early twentieth century. Farmers were required to keep horses and carrioles for travelers and tourists who, for a fee, would be transported to the next posting station. These were usually 6 to 8 miles apart. As late as 1900, there remained over 900 posting stations throughout Norway.

**A "lur" is a long, thin, horn-like wooden wind instrument common in Scandinavia. It was originally used to call to battle, but later used most commonly to call cows and for signalling across a distance.

But where are my thoughts?
I think about Anders, and long so to see him,
I think that he will never be mine.
Come *Mulros*, come *Svarti*,
come *Guldhorn* and *Bjelko*,
come here, you'll get salt.*
Anders is the handsomest boy in the valley.
He's the finest of all that I know.
He is faithful and honest,
and loves only me.

Scene 2: SNEFRID, ANDERS

SONG NUMBER 2

ANDERS *(enters, carrying a scythe)*
I am so tired of all the troubles everyday,
I wish I could simply leave.
Perhaps I'll cross the sea to find my fortune,
then return to take my Snefrid with.

SNEFRID
Yes, across the seas we'd travel if we could,
And live our happy lives in a distant woods.

(both of them)
There we'll work for our daily bread
and there we'll live in quiet peace.

SNEFRID
There we'll work and there we'll prosper
Even if we begin with nothing.

(both of them)
There we'll work for our daily bread
and there we'll live in quiet peace.

ANDERS Snefrid, I have so much to tell you today.

---

*In Norway, cows were taken to mountain farms for summer grazing where they were cared for by milk maids, young girls from farms in the area. In calling and keeping track of the cows, names were usually given to each animal.

SNEFRID When will we get a chance to talk together?

ANDERS You're right. We are watched all day as though we intended to do something wrong.

SNEFRID What can we do wrong if we love each other?

ANDERS No, there's nothing we can do wrong if we love the right person.

SNEFRID I know father has decided that I am to marry Ola because he has a farm, some land, and money in the bank.

ANDERS And I am just a simple cotter's son. I have no farm, no land, and no money in the bank. I have only my two arms. That's not enough for a farmer's daughter, I guess.

SNEFRID But you have the best anyway, Anders. You have a proper character and a good heart.

ANDERS God bless you, Snefrid. Every word like that you say to me gives me more strength and more courage. Sometimes, I fear that all the talk that I'm not good enough for you will wear you down and that you will marry a farmer with land and money in the bank instead of a simple cotter's son.

SNEFRID That's not nice of you to think, Anders. I haven't done anything to deserve so little faith in me.

ANDERS No, you haven't, Snefrid. I know it's not nice of me to think like that, but those thoughts just come and I can't do anything about it.

SNEFRID *(sighs)* I know. People can get many ideas and can't do anything about it. But tell me, Anders, do you intend to leave for America in the spring?

ANDERS Yes, it's the best thing for me. Staying here will lead to nothing more than inheriting the cotter's farm, and a family can't live off that. You've seen yourself how little can be earned from this farm and how poor we are.

SNEFRID Yes, yes, that's true. We may not be able to earn a living from that farm, but if you go to America, it'll take a long time before you can get anything like it, if at all.

ANDERS Oh, no! In Minnesota I can get government land—160 acres of good land—for free. As long as I work hard and save—

SNEFRID *(interrupts)* Yes, that I know you will.

ANDERS —then it won't take more than two years before we'll be able to make a living on the farm. Even if it's a little tight in the beginning, you'd accept that, wouldn't you?

SNEFRID Yes, of course, you know I don't require much.

ANDERS No, God knows you don't require much, at least now. But, don't you think it's the best thing if I go to America this spring?

SNEFRID I can't think of anything else. If it were possible to stay here, I would. It seems so strange to leave all relatives and friends. And the country over there is so different from here. The climate is different and strange there. One thrives best in conditions one has become used to.

ANDERS I agree with you, Snefrid. If I saw any possibility that I could become an independent, carefree man, I would rather stay home, too, but there is no such possibility for an ordinary workingman here in Norway. When have you seen a simple workingman become prosperous here? Here, it's a matter of: "To him who has, shall more be given, from him who does not have, shall more be taken away."* That's the way it is here in Norway; it's very nice for someone who already has, but for those who have nothing, it can be miserable. When it comes to the point where a laborer is barely more than an animal and has to take off his hat when talking with someone of a higher station, then all working people should consider getting out of this country. I want to get out of here, and I recommend that others do the same. I'm leaving this spring and I hope you will come a short while after that. Snefrid, do you promise me you will?

SNEFRID Yes, I promise, Anders!

SONG NUMBER 3

ANDERS

In a little cottage we will live,
in peace and quiet we'll love each other.
We'll teach our children

---

*See Matthew 13:12; 25:29; Mark 4:24–25; Luke 8:18; 19:26.

to honor God and the law,
and live in peace forever.

(both of them)

We'll teach our children
to honor God and the law,
and live in peace forever.

SNEFRID

In the beginning it may be humble,
but we have our love forever.
We'll live carefully
and have our love,
we'll have each other and our love forever.

(both of them)

We'll live carefully
and have our love,
we'll have each other and our love forever.

ANDERS

To America we will go.

SNEFRID

And I will follow where you go.

(both of them)

We will build a cottage
where we will live
with our love in our simple home.
And in the spring when we part,
You must promise to be faithful.
Faithful, with my love,
I promise you I'll always...
always think of you!

Scene 3: SNEFRID, ANDERS, HALVOR

SNEFRID Look, father is coming in from the field. Let him think I'm helping you with the sharpening stone.

(as Snefrid's father approaches, she turns the whetstone while Anders sharpens the scythe)

HALVOR *(to Anders)* Why are you standing there? Why aren't you out cutting hay, do you think it cuts itself?

ANDERS No, that's why I'm sharpening my scythe, so it'll cut much better.

HALVOR *(pulls Snefrid away from the whetstone)* It's none of your business to turn the whetstone. Go in and watch the porridge. Anders can take care of the sharpening. You better get to work, Anders, because all the grass needs to be cut today.

ANDERS *(picks up a small whetstone and continues sharpening)* As soon as I finish sharpening my scythe, I'll be able to get to the hay.

SONG NUMBER 4

ANDERS and SNEFRID

With patience
we'll reach
our final goal.
Yes, our final goal
we must keep in sight
without being dissuaded.
We are meant for each other,
meant for each other.

HALVOR

As soon as I get a chance
I will take care of this.
And do what I must
to see these two never one shall be.
I will soon see an end to this,
no, these two never a pair will be.
As sure as my name is Halvor,
let me tell you true,
that this girl, my daughter,
is too good for you.
Young people today are so unpractical.

Can they really live when the cupboard is bare?
Food is important in this life,
without, one can hardly live.
But without money, what will you do?
Love is fine, but one can't survive on that.
No, mark my words, this girl is too good for you.

Scene 4: HALVOR, SNEFRID

HALVOR Snefrid, I don't like that you talk so much to Anders.

SNEFRID I don't talk more with him than I do with others.

HALVOR Yes, you do. I fully understand that he's courting you and I also see that you like him. But, I tell you that nothing can come of it. Anders is nothing but a miserable cotter's son and that's nothing for a proper farmer's daughter like you. Ola is the right one for you; he's got a farm, land, and money in the bank. Do you hear me?

SNEFRID Yes.

HALVOR Now, I know you're reasonable and won't throw your life away on that miserable cotter's son. What do you think people would say about you? Do you think you could make a living on cotter's land that can barely feed two cows now? Or do you think you could survive on porridge and goat milk?

SNEFRID Well, if the cotter's land is too small for a family to live on, then I think it's your fault for not giving the cotter more land. It says in the scriptures that a worker is worth what you pay.

HALVOR Don't you bother yourself with what's in the scriptures; let that be a matter for the minister. You just worry about getting a husband who can provide properly for you and your children. When this little cotter's cottage is full of children, what will you do then? Don't think that you'll get anything from me.

SNEFRID No, I'd never think that.

HALVOR If you want to be crazy and throw away your life, don't think that I'll help you. Do you have anything to say to that?

SNEFRID *(remains silent)*

HALVOR Answer me. Don't stand there like some old cow!

SNEFRID I don't have anything to say.

HALVOR Well, you have to say something. I need to know before Ola asks me if it's all right for him to come courting you. I need to know what to tell him. Do you understand that?

(while Halvor is speaking, Guri comes out from the house)

SNEFRID No.

HALVOR No, yes, no, yes. Can't you open your mouth and answer properly?

SNEFRID I don't have anything to say.

HALVOR Well, by God, you better have something to say. I want to know, will you accept Ola or not?

SNEFRID I'm not so sure I want to get married at all.

HALVOR Not get married? What are you saying? What kind of talk is this? Are you planning to live at home all your life? No, that can't be true.

SNEFRID I'm thinking about going to America.

HALVOR Ha, ha, now I get it. Anders is going to America in the spring and you are planning to join him later. Well, at least I got to know it now, but it won't happen if I have any say in the matter. I don't ever want to see you with that cotter's son, you have nothing to gain from it. Now, you can do what you will, but I beg of you to consider what you're getting yourself into.

SONG NUMBER 5

HALVOR

More about this cotter's son,
I don't want to hear.
I have to teach you to obey
and you will do what I say
and take Ola,
he's the man for you.

SNEFRID

I hear what you tell me
but I won't look at what a man owns.
I don't care if he has a fortune to start,
for the one I want must have my heart.

HALVOR

What nonsense, do you think you could
live on only grass and mud?
No, my daughter will have a real man
with a farm, some land
and money in the bank.

(*Halvor and Snefrid together*)

SNEFRID

I don't care if he has a fortune,
I don't care for farm, land, or
money in the bank.

HALVOR

No, my daughter will have a man,
a proper man with farm, land, and
money in the bank.

HALVOR

Therefore Snefrid my advice to you
is accept a marriage that's best for you!

(*Halvor and Snefrid together*)

SNEFRID

Only they who know love, also know
that love's rules must be obeyed.

HALVOR

I know best from experience
my words to you must be
obeyed.

SNEFRID

Anders will be my husband.
It's him alone I love.
I will obey the rules of love,
for I understand what marriage
really is.

HALVOR

I tell you as sure as I live
that Anders you shall not have.
I am your father and I know best,
and understand what marriage
really is.

(they go into the house)

Scene 5: GURI, SNEFRID

GURI *(entered from the right near the end of the previous scene. She is sitting on a large rock, smoking a pipe)*

SNEFRID *(enters, sees Guri)* Hello, Guri.

GURI Good day, Snefrid.

SNEFRID How are you doing, Guri, enjoying your smoke?

GURI This is my last pipe, no more tobacco.

SNEFRID Well, here are two coins for more tobacco.

GURI Thank you, Snefrid, you're always so kind to me.

SNEFRID Unfortunately, I have so little to be kind with.

GURI I can't say my situation is any better.

SNEFRID Do you need a new pipe?

GURI Oh, no, old pipes are always best. As long as I have tobacco, I'm fine.

SNEFRID You'll always have tobacco. *(looks around)* No, you'll always have tobacco. *(looks around, again)* No, you won't lack for— *(looks around again, as though making sure no one is watching)* Guri?

GURI Yes?

SNEFRID You can predict the future, can't you?

GURI Yes, when I have a cup of good, strong coffee.

SNEFRID I'll get you one. Come on, come with me into the house. *(they go into the house to the left)*

Scene 6: OLA, HALVOR, GUNHILD, a TRAVELER

TRAVELER *(offstage)* Where is the groom for the horses? Hey! Groom! *(enters the stage)*

HALVOR *(comes out of the house)*

TRAVELER Can I get a horse, quickly? Can I get a horse?

HALVOR *(shouts out to the field)* Groom! Groom!

TRAVELER Damn! I'll be late to Lærdal and won't make the boat. Now, can I get a horse, quickly?

HALVOR Quickly? No, that's not possible. But now the groom's coming, so we can hear what he has to say.

OLA *(enters, out of breath)* Does somebody need a ride?

TRAVELER Yes, I must have a horse, immediately!

OLA That's not possible. With the exception of one, all of our horses are out and it's eight miles to the next station at Ole Brubakken's farm. So, it will take about three hours to get a horse.

TRAVELER It's not possible to wait three hours. That'll make me too late to Lærdal. Being just an hour late can cost me several hundred dollars.

HALVOR *(aside)* Well, this sounds to me as though we have one ready for plucking.

TRAVELER Are there no horses on the farm?

HALVOR Well, yes, we have one, but he is not required to be available for hire.

TRAVELER But, for crying out loud, you'll get paid well if I can use it anyway. I'll pay double the usual rate.

HALVOR Well, yes, I guess we could get a horse, if we come to some agreement.

TRAVELER You heard me. I'm willing to pay double the usual rate.

HALVOR That's very nice, but are you really in such a big hurry?

TRAVELER Don't you understand that I must be in a hurry, if I'm willing to pay twice as much as usual?

HALVOR Oh, yes, I can sort of understand it, but are you in such a hurry that you really want to exhaust the old nag?

TRAVELER I'm in a very big hurry!

HALVOR It's pretty hilly to the next posting station.

TRAVELER I know that.

HALVOR And the old nag can't stand to be overly exhausted.

TRAVELER No nag can stand that. Now, give me an answer, do I get a horse or not?

HALVOR To tell you the truth, I don't know.

TRAVELER *(to Ola)* Well, do you know?

OLA Me? No, I don't know anything.

TRAVELER You don't? Then you probably also don't know that you're a blockhead!

OLA Oh, yes, I do know that, because I hear others say it all the time.

TRAVELER *(to Halvor)* Listen, my good man, can I get a horse?

HALVOR It could be.

TRAVELER "It could be"? What the hell! When could it be? Soon?

HALVOR It could be.

TRAVELER *(stamps)* Unbelievable! Listen, could it be right now, this minute, if I paid you four times the usual rate?

HALVOR *(quickly to Ola)* Ola, get the horse and hitch it up to the carriole, quickly!

OLA *(runs out)*

HALVOR Hurry, Ola! *(shouts to Ola)* Don't take the nag, take the gray mare. Hurry, Ola!

TRAVELER Thank God, finally I'm getting a horse.

HALVOR But, you better be careful you don't wear out the mare. She's young and foolish, like yourself.

TRAVELER What did you say?

HALVOR I said, I think it's best that you pay for the ride beforehand.

TRAVELER No, I will not pay until I have reached the destination.

HALVOR *(shouts to Ola)* Ola! Take the harness off the mare!

TRAVELER No, no, no. Here's the money. *(pays)*

HALVOR *(shouts to Ola)* Ola! Put the harness on again.

TRAVELER How much is it?

HALVOR Oh, let's see, that'll be exactly— let me see— that's eight miles and six dollars for the horse, and one dollar for the carriole— that will be— seven dollars, times four, that will be— that will be—

TRAVELER Seven dollars?

HALVOR Is that it?

TRAVELER Yes, six and one is seven dollars.

HALVOR No, now wait a minute. You offered to pay four times the cost.

TRAVELER Yes, that's what it is. Four times the cost? Impudence if you ask me.

HALVOR Impudence? *(shouts to Ola)* Ola, take the harness off the mare.

TRAVELER No, no, it's not impudence, it's reasonable.

HALVOR Ola! Put the harness back on the mare.

TRAVELER Then it will be exactly twenty-eight dollars. Here you are. *(begins to count out the money)*

OLA *(offstage)* The gray mare is ready. She doesn't want to wait, are you ready to go?

TRAVELER *(speeds up the counting)* Ten dollars, fifteen, twenty-five, twenty-eight.

HALVOR Wait, stop.

TRAVELER No, do you want more?

HALVOR There is also a fifty-cent charge for ordering a ride.

TRAVELER But I didn't order a ride beforehand, I just arrived to ask for one.

HALVOR *(shouts out)* Ola, take—

TRAVELER *(interrupts and holds him back)* No, stop, stop, all right, here is fifty cents. Now, am I paid up?

HALVOR Well, not exactly, didn't we agree that you would pay four times the regular charge?

TRAVELER Now, this is impudent!

HALVOR *(starts to walk to the background to shout to Ola, but the traveler stops him and pays him)*

TRAVELER Here are two dollars. Now is everything paid?

HALVOR Yes, I think for the most, but you need to have a posting boy with you. *(shouts into the barn)* Gunhild, come out here!

GUNHILD *(comes out)* What is it?

HALVOR You'll have to go along with this man on the posting, "Little Ola" isn't here.

GUNHILD Then, can't "Big Ola" go along?

HALVOR No, *you* are to go along.

TRAVELER *(puts his arm around Gunhild's waist)* Come on along, Sweetie. We'll have a nice trip together.

GUNHILD Leave me alone.

TRAVELER Now, don't be so—

HALVOR *(to Gunhild)* You're too good for any fooling around? You usually aren't so particular. *(to the traveler)* You might be able to have some fun with the girl during the trip.

TRAVELER *(puts his arm around Gunhild's waist again)* We'll get along just fine. I always get along well with beautiful girls.

GUNHILD No, I don't want any part of anything like that. I'll get little Peer Nustua, he's out in the field. *(runs out)*

SONG NUMBER 6

TRAVELER

Damn, this is taking far too long
before I can get underway.

HALVOR

But later you travel so much faster,
o'er the mountains high.

OLA *(outside)*

The mare is ready,
it's time to go.

TRAVELER
Leaving in a hurry.

HALVOR
Arriving just in time.

TRAVELER
Would that it be soon.

GUNHILD *(enters with little Peer)*
Here is Peer, he'll travel with you.
He's the best to drive.

TRAVELER *(puts his arm around Gunhild's waist)*
I would rather you come along,
you're the driver I like best.

GUNHILD
No, with you I do not want to go.

OLA *(from outside)*
Hurry now, the mare is waiting.

GUNHILD and HALVOR
The mare is ready, can't you hear?
Hurry now, the road awaits.

OLA
The mare can fly,
but here's the whip in case of need.

TRAVELER
This mare will feel the whip.
I will use it well.

OLA and SNEFRID
But careful as you use the whip.
Careful, though you use it well.

HALVOR and GUNHILD
He cares nothing of the hills or roads,
as long as he makes the boat.

HALVOR, OLA, GUNHILD
Be careful, drive carefully.

The mare can be spooked.
Drive carefully, just don't be
too arrogant or proud.

TRAVELER

The horse will run like a hare,
no stone can spook the mare.
The only thing that matters
is getting to the boat on time.

(the traveler runs offstage with Peer and Halvor following)

Scene 7: OLA, GUNHILD

OLA *(begins to go into the house)*

GUNHILD Ola, there's something I have to talk to you about.

OLA Oh, what can that be?

GUNHILD You know very well.

OLA No, I don't have any idea.

GUNHILD Every Saturday night lately you've promised me that you were serious about me, but I'm beginning to think that you are playing me for a fool. I understand that you have begun to court Snefrid. Now, it might be that Snefrid is a nicer girl than I am, and she is the daughter of a well-off farmer while I'm just a simple girl, but that doesn't give you the right to make a fool of me. You can straight-out tell me if you don't want me, then I can at least find another. But one thing certain, you can forget about coming over on Saturday night.

OLA *(embarrassed)* What's gotten into you today?

GUNHILD I just want to know what's going to happen between us.

OLA Oh, that isn't so important is it?

GUNHILD Yes it is. Either you are faithful to me or to Snefrid.

OLA Well, if you want my opinion, I guess it's best that we no longer think about each other. I've gotten a promise from Snefrid and, truth be told, Snefrid is worth much more than you are.

GUNHILD I know that, but are you so sure that you'll get Snefrid?

OLA Oh, yes, Halvor has given me his word on it.

GUNHILD Has Snefrid given you her word on it?

OLA No, she hasn't, but she'll have to do what Halvor tells her.

GUNHILD That I don't think Snefrid will do. Anyway, she wants a man more elegant and smarter than you are.

OLA More elegant and smarter, you say? Am I not elegant or smart enough? Don't I have a farm, land, and money in the bank?

GUNHILD Yes, but it's not always money that makes the difference.

OLA And am I not smart enough for her?

GUNHILD Oh, you don't have a whole lot of sense, Ola. You know very well that people call you a half-wit. You're good enough for a simple girl like me, but Snefrid will have nothing to do with you, just you wait and see.

OLA Oh, you're a big cow!

GUNHILD And you're a big ox! *(she runs into the barn)*

OLA *(runs after her)*

GUNHILD *(slams the door before Ola gets to it)* You are a big ox!

OLA *(tries to open the door, but fails)* You just wait until I get hold of you. I'll give you a good going over, you'll see.

Scene 8: HALVOR, OLA

HALVOR What is the matter?

OLA Oh, nothing, but tell me, Halvor. What's going to happen between me and Snefrid?

(outside is heard the sound of a horse)

OLA Hey, here's another traveler.

HALVOR Maybe another one that I can squeeze for a few extra dollars. Come on, let's see who it is. *(goes out with Ola)*

Scene 9: GURI, GUNHILD

GURI *(comes out from the house)*

SONG NUMBER 7

GURI

When a women gets old and gray
and has reached her seventy years,
there is much she must endure
in wretched and miserable ways.
When a woman no longer can struggle,
then life itself ain't worth the living.
And by all she is scorned
as the lowest of the low,
and no one holds her dear.
And no one holds her dear.
Rejected, she rambles around,
occasionally thrown a coin.
Like a dog she goes round and round,
at a speed like a bat out of hell.
But the worst of all is the fix
that is there with no tobacco to mix.
For a pipe is a good friend, I say,
when you get to be old and gray.

GUNHILD *(comes out from the barn)*

Guri, I think you are grand,
and a quarter I put in your hand.

GURI

A quarter?
I thank you so much for the thought.

GUNHILD

Will you please tell me my fortune?

GURI

You want to know whom you will marry?

GUNHILD

Yes, I want to know.

GURI

And I can do that.

GUNHILD

Please tell me whom I shall marry.

GURI

Your fortune I can let you know.

GUNHILD

Will it be Ola I must marry at last?

GURI

I will be able to tell you whom you will marry.

GUNHILD

It's not good for young girls
who are being courted.
We believe in fortune-telling,
and in all this talk,
and pay with a bit of tobacco.

GURI

By roaming around and forecasting
the future for girls waiting and
being courted,
we give them nonsense
and a little talk,
and earn enough for a bit of tobacco.

GUNHILD Can you tell my fortune right now?

GURI I need a cup of strong coffee, you know.

GUNHILD You'll get it inside. I'll go put the coffee pot on. *(she goes into the house)*

Scene 10: GURI, SNEFRID, HALVOR

SNEFRID *(enters crying)*

GURI What's the matter, don't you like the fortune I predicted?

SNEFRID Oh yes, well— I don't know what I should say. But, Guri? I have such a pain in my chest. Can you help me with that?

GURI Well, I don't know. It isn't that long ago since I measured you. Didn't you feel better then?

SNEFRID Yes, I did, that's why I want you to measure me again. It helps a lot.

GURI Yes, I can measure you, but I'll need about six feet of wool thread, three teeth, and three coins.

SNEFRID I have everything ready. *(gives it to Guri)* See here, here it is.

GURI *(places the wool thread in a ring and lays the ring on the three teeth)* Spit three times through the ring.*

SNEFRID *(spits three times through the ring. Each time, Guri holds a coin underneath, which she, after each spitting, puts into her pocket. Then Guri makes the sign of the cross three times over the ring, and says:)*

GURI As I measure you, you are to repeat after me. *(measures her with the woolen thread)*

(both of them)

Branches, logs, sticks, and twigs,
a barnyard full of cows and pigs.
A one for me the best of all,
a man from Norway's Hallingdal.

(as they repeat the verse a second time, Halvor walks in. He listens in the background for a time, then rushes forward)

Scene 11: HALVOR, GURI, SNEFRID, GUNHILD

HALVOR *(angry)* What is going on here? I think you are practicing the magic of measuring. Don't you know that measuring, healing, locating lost things by magic, and performing any superstious act is forbidden by law and catechism? How can you presume to act like this, you old witch? I'm going to report you to the sheriff and he'll place you under arrest.

---

*Spitting three times is a ritual in several cultures usually intended to thwart evil or ensure the success of a spell. Spitting is said to chase the Devil and bad luck away. By crossing herself three times, Guri also invokes the assistance of the Christian god as a supplement to her superstitious beliefs. This "double-dipping" is not uncommon in the Norwegian folk tradition.

GURI I would thank you for that. That means I'll get better lodging than I'm getting by going around begging from farm to farm.

HALVOR Snefrid, why do you bother yourself with this witchcraft instead of doing something useful? Don't you think it's about time to get serious? Get your rake and go out to the field and help with the hay. And Gunhild? Where is she? *(tries the door to the house)* Gunhild! Are you standing there making coffee? Is this any time to be making coffee? Why are you making coffee now?

GUNHILD *(comes out of the house, embarrassed)* I— I—

HALVOR Why are you making coffee this time of the day?

SNEFRID I asked her to make coffee, because I—

HALVOR Shut up! Take your rakes and get to work!

(Snefrid and Gunhild go into the barn to get the rakes. They come out of the barn with the rakes, then go out in the background)

HALVOR *(to Guri)* And you? What are you doing here? Haven't you got what you came for?

GURI Yes!

HALVOR What are you waiting for then?

GURI For better times!

HALVOR You can talk. For you, there will be no better times.

GURI That's for God to decide. *(points to the heavens)*

HALVOR Oh sure, God doesn't have time to think about an old witch like you. An old woman like you should be satisfied with what you've got. Now, get out of here, and hurry!

GURI I don't hurry with anything.

HALVOR I believe that. Old women like you are best shot anyway. That's best for all the people who would otherwise have to feed you.

GURI But lead and powder costs money.

HALVOR You're right there, and you aren't worth the expense of a musket ball. I think I'll propose to the authorities that they take all old women like you and hang them in the highest trees. Ho, ho, ho, ho, that would be fun to see.

GURI You laugh heartily today, but she who laughs last, laughs best.

HALVOR Get out of here!

SONG NUMBER 8

HALVOR

See to it now that you get out of here
or else it won't go well for you.
I am not one to be fooled with
and that you will soon find out.

GURI

Oh, you don't have to threaten me,
if I want to stay here, then I will.
Don't think that you can frighten me.
I don't care what you say.

HALVOR

You old crones and heretics
should be done away with once and for all.
We should do as they did in the old days
and burn you witches at the stake.

GURI

You can recommend to all the authorities
that they burn old crones and heretics,
but we old women will not perish,
as sure as I'm standing here today.

HALVOR

What are you saying?

GURI

I'm telling the truth and nodding too.

HALVOR You old witch, I think I'll shoot you for standing there and teasing me.

GURI Don't bother using such harsh words; you bark, but you have no bite.

(Halvor gets angry, makes as though he will strike Guri, who runs out, chased by Halvor)

CURTAIN FALLS
END OF ACT I

Act II

Scene 1: HALVOR, OLA, LORD FITZGERALD

OLA *(outside)* Do you want a horse?

LORD *(outside)* No, no! I am not in a hurry!

HALVOR *(to himself)* Ho, ho, a traveling Englishman. Here's another I can pluck. Now there'll be some money to be made.

LORD *(enters with backpack, hunting gun, fishing pole, and wallet in his hand, writing on a pad, off and on)*

SONG NUMBER 9*

LORD

To be sure it is burdensome
to travel here in Norway's land,
but when I come to the mountains
there is pleasure enough at hand.

HALVOR

I don't understand.

OLA

I don't understand.

---

*In his original manuscript, Thrane has Lord Fitzgerald speaking a childish type of English, as though he would thereby be better understood by the Norwegians to whom he speaks. It is not clear if this is intended as parody or whether it was a reflection of Thrane's own poor command of English. While in Norway, Thrane probably encountered visiting Englishmen trying to make themselves understood by Norwegians by speaking a childlike English. As always in such instances, the misunderstandings of the language itself add to the humor of the situation.

LORD
I've come on a hunting expedition.

HALVOR and OLA *(to each other)*
I don't understand a word he's saying.

LORD *(writing)*
The people don't understand
that I want a man to guide me
while hunting and fishing.
A good man who would be willing
to leap o'er fearful stones and fences.

HALVOR
I don't understand.

OLA
I don't understand.

LORD
I've come on a hunting expedition.

HALVOR and OLA
I don't understand a word he's saying.

LORD *(writing)*
The people do look a little stupid.

HALVOR
Tell me, do you want a horse?
Then we'll get one right away.

LORD
No, no, no, no. No horse, no horse.
I want to hunt bears and fish salmon.

OLA
Now, I understand. He wants salmon.

HALVOR
You want salmon? We can get that for you right away.

LORD
I've come on a hunting expedition.

OLA and HALVOR *(to each other)*

I don't understand a word he's saying.

LORD *(writing)*

I don't like this place.
God damn, God damn. Don't you understand?
I want someone to go with me.
God damn, God damn, what a stupid country.

HALVOR

I don't understand.

OLA

I don't understand.

LORD

God damn, what can I do?

HALVOR

What the hell can he be saying?

LORD

Can I hunt here? Is there much fishing here?

HALVOR *(to Ola)*

What is it Ola?

OLA

Damned if I know what it is.

HALVOR

I think he's talking about fish.

LORD

Can I hunt here? *(makes the movement of shooting a rifle)*
Fishing here? *(makes the movement of casting a fishing line)*

HALVOR

I don't understand.

OLA

I don't understand.

LORD *(writing)* Their only answer is gibberish. *(aloud)* Fish! *(points to his mouth and then stomach, making a fishing movement)* Fish! Fish! God damn. Fish?

OLA He wants fish!

HALVOR Yes, indeed, he wants fish. Let's get the girls and they can make some fish for him. *(runs out with Ola)*

LORD *(writing)* They simply run away.

Scene 2: LORD FITZGERALD, HALVOR

HALVOR *(enters again)* I was to ask you for your payment for your ride from your posting driver.

LORD What? Now I don't understand.

HALVOR *(makes gesture of travel, horse, whip, and money)* Pay! Pay!

LORD Oh! Pay! Pay! Yes, pay! *(from his pocket, he takes a wad of money, reaches it to Halvor to allow him to take what it costs)* Here is payment!

HALVOR *(to himself)* Ho, ho! It looks like he calculates very well. I think there can be some money to be made here. Let me see, now. The posting driver should have two dollars. I can easily take an extra dollar for the trouble. It's no sin to take from such a rich Englishman. *(takes more)* Now I earned an extra dollar. *(to the Lord)* That's right! *(nods to the Lord and goes)*

LORD *(looks at his money, then writes)* At this station the landlord cheated me immediately for one dollar.

HALVOR *(back again, to himself)* Damn if there isn't plenty to pump here. I'm going to pump him real good.

Scene 3: LORD FITZGERALD, GUNHILD, SNEFRID, OLA, HALVOR

OLA *(outside)* There's a rich Englishman out here who wants some fish.

GUNHILD There is no fish here.

OLA *(enters with Gunhild and Snefrid)* We'll have to get some fish if we're going to— I don't know what—

HALVOR Hi, girls! You have to make some fish for the Englishman. He wants fish and he has lots of money to pay for it.

SNEFRID We can't make any fish until it's been fished, but it wouldn't take much to catch a couple of trout.

HALVOR Yes, Ola, let's take a couple of fishing poles and it won't be long before we get some fish. *(runs out with Ola)*

LORD *(to Gunhild)* I am very thirsty, I want some milk to drink.

GUNHILD Ha, ha, ha. You better speak Norwegian. Because I don't know what you're saying.

LORD Milk. Milk. *(makes a drinking motion)*

GUNHILD Oh, now I understand. You want milk. *(she runs out to the barn)*

LORD *(writes)* Hmmmm. At last she understands me; she was not very pretty, but the other girl is very pretty. *(to Snefrid)* What is your name?

SNEFRID What? I don't understand you.

LORD Your name. Do write your name here. *(hands her a pencil and the paper)*

SNEFRID Oh, now I understand. *(she writes)*

LORD *(looks at it)* Oh, my God! That is splendid! *(writes)* She wrote her name very nicely in my book; she is very beautiful. *(to Snefrid)* Will you please to give me a kiss?

SNEFRID What?

LORD A kiss, a kiss. *(makes a kissing motion)*

SNEFRID Oh, you want a kiss. Ha, ha, ha.

LORD Yes, yes, a kiss.

SNEFRID I don't know how to kiss in English.

LORD A kiss?

SNEFRID Oh, yes, you can have that, you look like a nice person. *(kisses him)*

LORD *(makes smacking sound)* Ah! Ah! Very good, indeed very good. *(writes)* The beautiful Snefrid consented to give me a kiss. That was the best kiss I ever got in my life. *(to Snefrid)* Look here, take ten dollars for that kiss.

SNEFRID Ha, ha, ha, ha. No, no.

LORD *(writes)* She refused ten dollars. *(to Snefrid)* Look here, take 100 dollars!

SNEFRID *(takes the bill, looks at it)* Oh, my God, I wish I could keep this money! But, I can't. No, no. *(gives the money back)* No, I can't sell a kiss.

LORD *(takes the money back and writes)* Wonder of wonder! She even refused 100 dollars!

GUNHILD *(enters with a bucket of milk and offers him a drink from the bucket)*

LORD Ha, ha, ha. *(writes)* She offered me a bucket full of milk. *(drinks)*

Scene 4: LORD FITZGERALD, SNEFRID, GUNHILD, OLA, HALVOR

OLA and HALVOR *(enter, each carrying a fish)*

HALVOR You'll pay a dollar for this one, I take it.

LORD No, no. I don't want fish in this way. I want someone to go with me on a hunting and fishing expedition.

ALL I don't understand.

LORD Gracious God! Nobody understands.

SNEFRID Father, you know that Anders wants to go to America in the spring.

HALVOR Yes, I know that. I also know that it would be best if he went tomorrow.

SNEFRID Well, for the past half year, Anders has studied English. His teacher has worked with him and it's possible that Anders can understand the Englishman.

HALVOR Damned if you aren't right. *(shouts out to the farmyard)* Anders! An...ders!

ANDERS *(answers in the distance)* Y...e...s.

HALVOR Come here...and...speak English!

SNEFRID *(to Lord Fitzgerald)* Now there's a fellow coming who knows English. Then we'll be able to understand you.

LORD What?

SNEFRID Man! Coming! English! Speak!

LORD Oh, finally someone who speaks English. Very well.

Scene 5: LORD FITZGERALD, SNEFRID, GUNHILD, OLA, HALVOR, ANDERS

ANDERS *(enters carrying a scythe)*

HALVOR Don't you speak English, Anders?

ANDERS Oh, not much. But the teacher has worked with me lately so I do know a little.

HALVOR Talk with this Englishman then!

ANDERS *(to Lord Fitzgerald)* What do you want?

LORD *(happy)* You speak English, oh, I am very glad; *(writes)* at last. Hmmm. I will tell you. I want someone to go with me on a hunting and fishing expedition. I am willing to pay exceedingly well. Will you go with me?

HALVOR *(to Anders)* What does he say?

ANDERS He wants me to go fishing and hunting with him. He will pay well, he says.

HALVOR Ask him how much he'll pay.

ANDERS What pay you for day?

LORD I will give you two dollars a day.

ANDERS *(to Halvor)* He'll pay me two dollars a day.

HALVOR That's good. Tell him you'll go with.

ANDERS *(to Lord)* Yes!

LORD All right! Make yourself ready! Take a gun with you and come along. *(writes)* At last I got someone who speaks a little English.

ANDERS *(goes in to get his rifle and his bag)*

OLA What is it he's always writing?

GUNHILD That, I would also like to know.

SNEFRID I think he's writing everything we say and do. *(to Anders)* Anders, ask him what he keeps writing in his book.

ANDERS What write you in that book?

LORD I put down all that I hear and see.

ANDERS Yes, he writes everything he sees and hears.

GUNHILD Tell him, he can't write anything in there about me.

SNEFRID And not me either!

ANDERS *(to Lord)* You must not write up what the girls say.

LORD Ha, ha, ha, ha. *(writes)* The girls are afraid of my putting down their doings and sayings.

ANDERS Englishman! I am ready!

LORD Are there many bears in the forest?

ANDERS Yes, many!

LORD Are you acquainted with bear hunting?

ANDERS Yes, a great bear is now in the forest. A very wild bear.

LORD All right! Then I like the bear and will talk with him. *(writes and looks around)*

HALVOR What's he saying?

ANDERS He wants me go with him to hunt a bear first.

OLA Yes, the forest has a very big bear.

HALVOR Yes, the one that Ola Langbein was hunting.

OLA Exactly.

SNEFRID But that bear tore apart and killed a man.

GUNHILD Yes, that's right, he tore apart Ola Langbein.

SNEFRID Anders, don't hunt that bear.

HALVOR *(to Snefrid)* Shut up! What's it got to do with you?

SNEFRID Anders, don't go! Don't go!

ANDERS Don't worry, Snefrid, there's no danger to me.

SNEFRID You say that, but Ola Langbein said the same thing. He didn't think there was any danger either.

OLA It's amazing how sensitive you are about Anders, Snefrid.

GUNHILD *(to Ola)* Oh, Snefrid is sensitive about all people.

OLA Nobody's talking to you, Gunhild.

GUNHILD Don't I have the right to talk to you?

ANDERS *(to Snefrid)* Don't worry, Snefrid. I'll come back home in as good shape as I am leaving.

SNEFRID But Anders, I'm so afraid.

HALVOR *(to Anders)* Anders, you have to be a man and not let yourself get scared by these women.

ANDERS Let me worry about that.

HALVOR *(slowly to Ola)* I think that Anders might not come back home in one piece.

OLA Why not?

HALVOR You know how foolhardy he can be. If he behaves on this bear hunt like he's done before, it won't go well for him. And I wouldn't really mind if the bear tore him into a hundred pieces.

OLA I wouldn't have anything against that either, he's such a big nosey good-for-nothing!

HALVOR and OLA Maybe by sunset, he'll be dead. I'm sure he will never return.

SNEFRID and GUNHILD God, please protect him. I can't relax until he's back and we are together, safe at home.

ANDERS I will not miss. The bear will fall. I will return safely home again.

LORD The bear will soon meet his death. And now, up to the mountains to kill the dreadful bear!

(Anders and Lord Fitzgerald leave)

Scene 6: OLA, HALVOR, GURI, SNEFRID, GUNHILD

HALVOR *(to Ola)* Well, now we're rid of Anders for awhile; maybe we're rid of him for good.

OLA I wouldn't be surprised. That bear up there in the woods is so bloodthirsty that no one can get away from him.

HALVOR Listen here, Ola, I have something to tell you. *(takes him aside)*

SNEFRID *(to Gunhild)* I'm so afraid. I feel as though something is telling me that something bad is going to happen to Anders during this hunt.

GUNHILD Oh, don't worry, Snefrid. Anders is the bravest boy in the whole area. He'll manage just fine.

SNEFRID I hope you're right.

HALVOR What are you doing standing around, girls? Get out there and take in the hay!

(Gunhild and Snefrid leave carrying the rakes. As they leave, they meet Guri. They make a sign to her and give her some coins)

Scene 7: OLA, HALVOR, GURI

OLA Halvor, tell me, what's going to happen between me and Snefrid?

HALVOR It'll be just as I've said.

OLA Well, that's well enough, but what hasn't been said is if Snefrid will go along with it.

HALVOR No, I'm afraid of that. I don't know what to do with that girl. She seems to be totally bewitched by Anders.

OLA Yes, I'm pretty sure that there's already something between them.

HALVOR Well, I'd much prefer that you get Snefrid, Ola, because you are established with a farm and land. This cotter's son, however, will only lead her into poverty and misery. But tell me, couldn't we come up with a remedy?

OLA I guess we could come up with a list of things.

HALVOR But what could that be?

OLA I don't know. *(looks around)* Hey, look! There's Guri.

GURI *(has stood watching, but now comes forward)* Here comes the old witch again.

OLA *(to Halvor)* Do you think we could talk with Guri?

HALVOR What good would that do?

OLA You know that the girls really believe in Guri. She's able to tell the future, perform healing, and she knows the art of black magic too. If we give her a couple of coins for tobacco and a new pipe, we could get her to predict bad things for Snefrid if she insists on having Anders.

HALVOR That doesn't sound so stupid, you know. I think we ought to do that. Guri!

GURI Yeh?

HALVOR Here's some change for you, for tobacco.

OLA Here's some from me, too.

GURI *(without looking at them, takes the money)* Thank you!

HALVOR Guri, don't you tell people's fortune and do black magic?

GURI People tell fortunes, but God decides all.

HALVOR Yes, I know that well enough, but some people know more than others.

OLA And I understand, Guri, that you know much more than either of us.

GURI Seventy years knows more than fifty years, and fifty years knows more than thirty.

HALVOR Could you do me a favor? I'll pay you well, you know.

GURI Well, perhaps.

HALVOR I understand that Snefrid likes Anders and that there's something between them. Couldn't you use some of your fortune-telling and black magic to get Snefrid away from Anders? Anders is only a poor cotter's son who has nothing and is not the right person for Snefrid.

OLA Can you do it, Guri? Why don't you answer?

GURI I want to think about how best to do this.

HALVOR You're right, Guri. *(claps his hands)* You won't regret it. Here's some money, and you'll get some from Ola too.

OLA Here's a dollar from me.

HALVOR That's right, Ola. Now, Guri, haven't we been nice to you? That'll give you tobacco for a long time yet. Now, let's see that you appreciate what we've done for you.

OLA Now, let's see. You are to make Snefrid so scared that she will change to what is right. You can use all the black magic you know.

(a lur is heard in the distance)

HALVOR The girls are coming. Predict all kinds of bad things for them. We'll stand here in the barn and listen.

(Ola and Halvor go into the barn, hold the door slightly open and look out, listening. A lur is heard in the background. Snefrid comes down from the mountains with the lur and the milk pail. It is beginning to be dusk. Guri has been inside to get a cup of coffee. She sits on a stone and drinks. Snefrid comes closer)

Scene 8: GURI, SNEFRID, GUNHILD, OLA, HALVOR

SNEFRID *(with trembling voice)* Are you there, Guri?

GURI Yes.

SNEFRID I'm so afraid today.

GURI Only the Evil One has reason to be afraid.

SNEFRID It's so dark, it looks like bad weather is coming.

GURI God decides the wind and the rain, and the fate of humanity.

SNEFRID Oh, if only I knew my fate!

GURI Hm!

SNEFRID What do you have in your cup?

GURI Coffee.

SNEFRID Drink it.

GURI *(drinks from the cup)* Now it's empty. *(overturns the cup and places it on the stone)*

SNEFRID *(takes the cup and looks into it. Recitative:)*
No, it's also dark for me

for one her fate to see.
And it must be that way,
much more than I can know.
As though bad luck's ahead for me,
but that much now I don't know,
I've never felt this way before.
Guri, you are old, but wise and true,
won't you tell me what it means?
Tell me what my fate will be.

(it becomes darker; lightning flashes)

SNEFRID *(screams slightly and covers her eyes)* Oh, God, what can this be? Tell me, Guri, is it a sign of something bad? *(frightened, Snefrid grabs Guri)*

(music in the background)

GURI *(takes the cup from Snefrid and looks into it. Recitative:)*
See here, here are many roads
with many curves;
by the side of the road is a very deep ditch,
perilous for those who travel.
The gentle and the good need not fear
they will reach their goal.
No matter how dark it may seem,
the pious always serve their God.

(after the recitative, a shot is heard in the distance. Thereafter lightning and thunder. Another shot and the cry of "Help!" is heard far away)

SNEFRID *(throws herself on her knees and begins to pray)*

GUNHILD *(comes running in, confused)* Someone is shouting for help up in the forest. There must be an accident. *(shouts)* Ola! Halvor! Come! Come! Somebody in the forest needs help. *(she runs into the house looking for them, but comes right back. As she closes the door, she sees Ola and Halvor)* Why are you just standing there?

SNEFRID Father! Ola! Make yourselves useful! There's been some kind of accident in the forest!

(thunder and lightning. Another cry for help. Ola and Halvor run out of the barn)

OLA What do we do now, Halvor?

HALVOR I don't know.

SNEFRID Run up to the forest as quickly as you can. Do something!

OLA *(to Halvor)* Maybe it's not Anders who needs help, maybe it's the Englishman.

HALVOR Yes, maybe that's it. And if we could help the Englishman, there's bound to be some money to be made. Good thinking, Ola! *(Halvor and Ola run off to go up the mountain to the forest)*

Scene 9: SNEFRID, GURI, GUNHILD, (later) ANDERS

SONG NUMBER 10

Verse 1: Prayer

GURI, GUNHILD, and SNEFRID *(Guri stands with arms raised, Gunhild with hands folded, and Snefrid on her knees)*

Stand by us, almighty Father,
and help us in our hour of need.
You do not forsake your children
or let the pious perish.
Be merciful to us, Oh Lord,
and hear our faithful prayer.
Protect us always, humbly
we pray to the Lord God, your son.

Verse 2:

MALE CHORUS *(heard in the distance)*

This hunt has proved dangerous, for
dangerous is the bear in the forest.
We must carry the wounded home gently,
or his life it will be in danger.

FEMALE CHORUS

Be merciful to us, Oh Lord,
and hear our faithful prayer.

Protect us always, humbly
we pray to the Lord God, your son.

MALE CHORUS

This hunt has proved dangerous, for
dangerous is the bear in the forest.
We must carry the wounded home gently,
or his life it will be in danger.

Verse 3:

MALE CHORUS *(still offstage)*

Severely wounded,
carefully carried home
if he is to be saved
from the threat.
We must try,
we must try.

Home, we bring him
to care for him there.
Then he'll be saved
and very soon well.
Within a week
the danger'll be over.
Down the mountain
we carefully carry
to ease the pain.

(they come down from the mountain, carrying Lord Fitzgerald on a stretcher)

Verse 4:

SNEFRID, GURI, GUNHILD

Oh, thank God.
He isn't hurt.

OLA and HALVOR

He'll realize what we did
and reward us.

SNEFRID, GURI, GUNHILD

A decent bed must be made ready.
We must do all we can for him.

OLA and HALVOR

There's money to be made here.

SNEFRID, GURI, GUNHILD, and ANDERS

We must bandage his wounds.

ALL

We must do all we can to save him.

ANDERS

The fight was enormous! And I was quite lucky.

SNEFRID

Thanks be to God that we see you safe again.

ALL

The fight for the booty is over.
Now we must do all we can to save him.

(end of song)

HALVOR *(to Ola)* Now there's some money to make. After we've nursed him back to health and he's well again, he'll spread money all over. Then we'll finally be able to rid ourselves of Anders.

LORD *(lying on the stretcher, raises himself slightly)* God damn! That is too bad! Damned bear! Anders!

ANDERS What?

LORD My book? I will write.

ANDERS You cannot write now.

LORD I will! Give me my book. *(falls back)* Ow! Ow!

ANDERS *(takes the book out of his pocket, with a pencil, and gives it to him)*

LORD *(raises himself again, writes a little)* And having discharged both our guns, we were defenseless. The bear then— *(falls back again)*

ANDERS You see, you cannot write.

LORD Well! Then I'll write tomorrow— aaaaa— I— want—a— aaa— I want *(voice weakens)* I want a— a— a—

OLA He's fainted!

HALVOR Yes, damned if he hasn't fainted. Why did you let him write, Anders? Get away! I'll take care of him myself. We'll take him into the house. Come and help me carry him in.

OLA *(goes to help)*

LORD No. No, God damn. Not into the house. It reeks of smelly cheese.

HALVOR *(to Anders)* What's he saying?

ANDERS He says, he doesn't want to be carried into the house because it smells too much like *Gammelost*.*

HALVOR Oh, really? Does he say it smells like *gammelost* in there?

LORD Oh! Oh! Oh!

OLA Listen, he wants to say something.

ANDERS *(listens to him)* What do you want?

LORD *(slowly in Anders's ear)* I want a kiss.

ANDERS Ha, ha, ha, ha. Thank goodness. He'll live, he wants a kiss.

OLA If that's what he wants, that's what he'll get. *(wipes his mouth and gets ready for a kiss)*

LORD *(strikes him so he falls backwards with his legs in the air)*

HALVOR Gunhild, you better give him a kiss.

LORD No. No, Snefrid— kiss.

ANDERS It's you, Snefrid, who he wants to kiss.

SNEFRID *(kisses him)*

LORD *(smacks)* Ah, that was splendid! Ah! I feel better now. *(raises himself)* Yes, much better— indeed! Snefrid! You are a first-rate doctor! You might graduate at any time. *(wants to get up)*

**Gammelost* is, literally, "old cheese" and is a specific type of cheese. I have chosen to use the term "smelly cheese" simply because it conveys Thrane's intent without presuming a familiarity with the type of cheese itself. It is a fully matured, highly pungent sour milk cheese that was very common and popular in Norway in the nineteenth century.

HALVOR *(tries to force him down again)* No, you must not try to stand up yet.

LORD *(pushes Halvor away)* Get away! I know very well what I am doing. Anders!

ANDERS What?

LORD Tell the story. The whole story.

SNEFRID What's he saying?

ANDERS He wants me to tell what happened on the hunt.

GUNHILD and SNEFRID Yes, tell us.

ANDERS Well, there isn't much to tell. We came across the same bear that tore Ola Langbein to pieces last spring. First we shot at him, but missed. The second shot wounded him in the leg and the bear became very angry. He charged the Englishman and seemed ready to tear him to pieces when I grabbed the bear in his hindquarters—you know how sensitive the bear is in his rump. When he realized that someone was holding into his backside, he released the Englishman to get hold of me. Now all this was happening right by the edge of the cliff, and as the bear started to turn, I pushed him so that he tumbled over the edge and down the mountainside. He must have hit himself pretty hard because he lay still for a long time, just groaning.

LORD *(during Anders's explanation, he has been writing furiously)* He saved my life. Say, Anders! Wouldn't you like to go with me?

ANDERS I don't know.

LORD If you don't know, I don't know either.

ANDERS What?

LORD I want you to travel with me everywhere—everywhere. You know, to Finmark, Lapland, Russia, Turkey, Italy, Africa—everywhere.

ANDERS No, no.

LORD Why not?

ANDERS I don't want to leave here.

LORD Why not?

ANDERS Hm— hm— aa—

LORD Well, I think I know! I suppose you like a certain girl, isn't that so?

ANDERS Yes, I guess that's it.

LORD Do you plan to marry the girl?

ANDERS *(sighs)* I'm afraid I'm too poor for that.

LORD Too poor, you say?

ANDERS Yes, too poor.

LORD You are not poor, my boy. *(to Halvor)* Are you the father of this girl?

HALVOR What?

ANDERS He's asking if you're Snefrid's father.

HALVOR Yes, I should think so!

LORD You like money, I suppose?

ANDERS He's asking if you like money.

HALVOR Hell, yes!

LORD *(writing)* Hmmmm. He answered: "Hell, yes." *(to Anders)* Ask him if he is willing to sell the girl.

ANDERS He's asking if you're willing to sell the girl.

HALVOR Sell the girl, you say? Is he crazy? Ask him what he means.

LORD I will pay 2000 dollars for the girl.

ANDERS He will give you 2000 dollars for Snefrid.

HALVOR 2000 dollars, you say? What did you say, 2000 dollars? That's a beautiful amount of money. For 2000 dollars, I could buy two farms and a large forest as well. Then I could live like a king. But I can't sell my daughter! What do you say, Snefrid? We can't do that in a Christian country. What would people say?

SNEFRID *(to Anders)* I well understand the Englishman's intention. *(to Halvor)* Yes, Father, I think we can do that if I agree to it.

HALVOR Are you willing to agree to it?

SNEFRID Yes, if he's willing to treat me as his own daughter.

HALVOR Ask him, Anders.

ANDERS Will you treat her as a daughter?

LORD Of course; just like my own daughter.

ANDERS *(to Halvor)* Yes, exactly like his own daughter, he says.

SNEFRID Do you hear that, Father? When a rich man like that wants to assume responsibility for me as his own daughter and give me a good education, wouldn't you be happy about that, even if you didn't get any money?

HALVOR Yes, you bet!

SNEFRID Well, so much the better now that you get some money as well.

HALVOR Yes, you're right there, but it's so strange to sell you, for money.

SNEFRID Well, it's not really selling me, you see. First, you give me to him. Then, because you are now related, he gives you 2000 dollars.

HALVOR Yes, that's right, Snefrid. You're a smart girl. It's not like I'm selling you for money, but as your father, I'm looking out for my daughter's best interests.

SNEFRID Of course.

OLA But, Halvor, was this your intention?

HALVOR Shut up! *(to Anders)* Anders, explain this to the Englishman.

ANDERS He will give you Snefrid as a present. After that you'll give him 2000 dollars as a present.

LORD Ha, ha, ha. Yes, all right—here is 2000 dollars.

HALVOR Damn! I've never seen that much cash at one time! And here is the girl as a present—as a present, you understand!

LORD Now, you are my daughter *(kisses her on the forehead)* and I will give you 2000 dollars as a present. As a present, you know. *(gives the money)*

HALVOR That was quite a transaction. Oh, if only I had several other daughters.

LORD *(to Anders)* Well, my dear Anders. As far as I understand, you like my daughter, isn't that so?

ANDERS Yes, that is so.

LORD Well, I give you my daughter as a present. *(gives her)*

ANDERS and SNEFRID *(throw their arms around him, kissing him on his cheeks)* Thank you! Thank you! Thank you!

OLA What the devil is going on?

HALVOR What is this? What is the meaning of this? *(wants to take Snefrid back)* I'll be damned if I agree to this.

LORD *(pushes him good-naturedly back)* This is my business. I am the father of the girl. *(to Anders)* And now, I will tell you: I will give you 2000 as a present. Then you can buy a farm and marry the girl. *(gives him the money)*

ANDERS and SNEFRID *(throw themselves around the Lord's neck and kiss him)*

LORD Ow! Ow! You're killing me! *(writes)* There were no bounds to their happiness; they almost killed me with embraces and kisses.

ANDERS *(waving the money in the air)* Hurrah! Now, I'm a rich man. I've gotten the prettiest girl in the district and 2000 dollars.

HALVOR Anders, you know, I've actually liked you better than the other boys in the district.

ANDERS No, is that true?

HALVOR Yes, damned if it isn't true. I've always thought how remarkable it would be to see you and Snefrid together, that's what I've thought.

ANDERS No, is that really true?

HALVOR Yes, damned if it isn't true. Come on, let me give you a hug. *(he hugs him)*

OLA *(scratches his head)* This is not working out right. This is a cheat and a swindle. It is a vile world we live in. But it's not going to exploit me anymore. Snefrid doesn't want me, Halvor will have nothing to do with me. Things look bleak for me if I'm going to find a wife. I mean, well, at least there's Gunhild anyway. *(to Gunhild)* Gunhild, will you be my wife?

SNEFRID *(pushes Ola away)* No, Gunhild! Don't take Ola. Anders and I will give you a decent dowry and you can get a much more handsome man.

OLA Now, Gunhild, how I want you to be my wife. Do you hear?

GUNHILD *(to Ola)* I thank you, Ola, but I have reconsidered.

OLA What? Now I don't get her either.

GURI I'm best suited to be your wife, Ola.

OLA *(pushes her away)* Oh, go to hell, you witch!

ANDERS Guri, here are five dollars for tobacco.

SNEFRID And now, Guri, we're buying a farm and you can be with us on the farm for as long as you live. And you'll be able to drink coffee all day.

GURI *(places her hands on Anders and Snefrid's heads)* God bless you both!

SONG NUMBER 11

Verse 1:

HALVOR

This day has been good to me,
two thousand dollars have I earned.
An Englishman is rather strange
to pay as much as he did and
throw his money around like grass.
The master doesn't need the money.

LORD *(writes)*

The master doesn't need the money.

Verse 2:

OLA

I think I will never get married,
or at least, I'll be one of the last.
No one, it seems, will have me.
Am I destined to be all alone?
Had I not been such a blockhead

and behaved as badly as I did
Gunhild might have said yes, after all.

LORD *(writes)*
Gunhild might have said yes, after all.

Verse 3:

GURI
Now I won't have to beg
and go from farm to farm.
Tobacco and coffee for me,
gone is my time without.
But if anyone wants
their fortune be told,
I'll do the best I can.

LORD *(writes)*
She'll do the best she can.

Verse 4:

ANDERS and SNEFRID
Happiness is always there
for two who are truly in love.
For true love will always win out
and be rewarded the best that you know.
Even if it looks dark,
if you believe in the God of love,
the end will bring light to us all.

LORD *(writes)*
The end will bring light to us all.

Verse 5:

GUNHILD
It happens that sometimes we don't win,
such as when I no husband could find.
But with a little patience
I'll find one better next time.

So even if things appear bleak,
the best will happen, you'll see,
if you only believe that it can.

LORD *(writes)*

If you only believe that it can.

Verse 6:

LORD

I'll write as fast as I can,
putting down what is worthy of mention.
To be sure, in every country
there is something worthy of attention.
For instance, the play tonight.
Does the audience think it was right?
If so, I'll write it down now.

(points to his book and pencil)

Verse 7:

ALL

Far away in a mountainous land
there are many interesting stories.
In those mountains there are
more stories than anyone could guess.
So be happy and glad
that our story ended as well
as it did here for us tonight.

CURTAIN FALLS

THE END

Who Grinds the Coffee?

A COMEDY IN ONE ACT

Characters:

PETER

MARIE, his wife

FREDERIK

SOFIE, his fiancé

Setting:
A simple one-room house with a back door.
A bed to the left and an oven to the right.

Scene 1: PETER, MARIE

PETER *(puts wood on the fire, pours water into the coffee pot)* Now that it's nice and warm here, I can wake up my wife. *(goes over to the bed where Marie is sleeping)* Marie! Marie! *(louder)* Marie! Marie!

MARIE *(yawning)*

PETER Marie! You have to get up. It's six o'clock! *(points to the clock on the wall)*

MARIE Shhhh... *(yawns)*

PETER It's six o'clock. Do you hear me? *(points)* You have to get up now!

MARIE Shhhh... Don't bother me.

PETER *(shakes his head. Walks over to the stove where he blows on the fire. Opens the top of the coffee pot to see if the water is boiling)* She's fast asleep and won't let me wake her up. Well, well. Times do change and we have to change with them. It wasn't too long ago that the wife got up at five o'clock and the husband stayed in bed until the room was warm and the coffee was ready. But now it's the husband who has to get up while the wife sleeps until six o'clock waiting for the room to be comfortable. It's America's fault! All these letters from America have made women downright rebellious. Her sister writes in one letter after another about how splendid it is for a woman in America. There they don't have to get up to light the fire, they don't have to milk the cows, and they don't have to shine shoes if they don't want to. And they don't want to! They don't even want to take care of children, and all this in the name of emancipation! If it continues to be like this, God only knows what will happen to men. Damn this America!

MARIE *(snores)*

PETER Oh, yes, it's edifying to listen to. Now she's falling asleep again and I'll never get her up. No, this is unacceptable. *(looks at his watch)* Ten minutes past six! *(goes over to the bed and shakes her slightly in the arm)* Marie! Marie! You have to get up, it's ten past six.

MARIE Shhhh... Leave me alone.

PETER But, you have to get up.

MARIE Quiet! Let me just finish my dream first.

PETER Is it a long dream?

MARIE Stop talking!

PETER If you don't get up now, I'll be late for work.

MARIE Shhhh...

PETER No, this is very confusing. Is it going to be like this every morning? It's America's fault! Oh, to be rid of America!

Scene 2: PETER, MARIE, SOFIE

SOFIE *(outside, knocking)*

PETER Come in!

MARIE *(sits up in the bed)* Are you crazy? You can't let anyone in while I'm still in bed.

PETER Well, why don't you get up then? *(goes to the door)* Don't come in! Don't come in!

SOFIE Oh, open the door, it's only me.

PETER Who me?

SOFIE Me, Sofie!

PETER Oh, is it you? *(opens the door)*

SOFIE But, my God, Marie? Are you still in bed? It's almost seven o'clock.

MARIE Seven o'clock, are you crazy? But Peter, what are you thinking? Why didn't you wake me before? You're going to be late for work again.

PETER Well, if you hurry up and make some coffee, I'll get to work in time.

MARIE Yes, I'm getting up. *(gets up)* Peter, take the coffee grinder and grind some coffee while I get dressed. *(begins to dress herself)*

PETER Grind coffee? Do you want me to grind coffee now, too?

MARIE Yes, you've got plenty of time.

PETER But, grind coffee? That's your job, not mine.

MARIE Nonsense, just hurry up.

PETER *(takes a tin of coffee beans, puts them into a coffee grinder, and seats himself to begin to grind. Reconsiders and sets the grinder on the table)* No, I swear, I am not going to grind the coffee.

MARIE *(looks at him, quietly and stiffly)* What are you doing?

PETER I don't want to grind the coffee.

MARIE You don't want to?

PETER Right, I do not want to.

MARIE Really? *(quietly seats herself)*

PETER *(looks at her)*

MARIE *(looks at him again)*

PETER So, what's up?

MARIE You don't want to?

PETER Nope!

MARIE Really? Hm! La, la, la, la, la, la.

PETER La, la, la, la, la.

MARIE You're cheerful today, Peter!

PETER Yes, when you're cheerful, I'm cheerful.

MARIE I am not cheerful, my friend.

PETER Me neither, my friend.

MARIE So, you don't want to grind coffee?

PETER Nooo!

MARIE Well, then you might as well go to work without breakfast.

PETER You'll actually let me go to work without breakfast?

MARIE Yes, since you don't want any.

PETER No, this is too much. *(picks up the grinder, but changes his mind and sets it down again)* No, I will not!

MARIE La, la, la, la.

PETER *(mimics Marie's voice)* La, la, la, la. Listen here, Marie. Who is the man in this house?

MARIE Who's the man? Don't you know that?

PETER No, I don't think I do.

MARIE Then, I don't know either. But I do know that I am the woman in this house.

PETER It sounds as though you know you are the woman here, and if you know that, then you should also know that it's your duty to see to it that breakfast is served.

MARIE I will see to it that breakfast is served, after you grind the coffee.

PETER I will not, I tell you.

MARIE All right. La, la, la, la.

PETER *(hums)* Oh, marriage, oh, marriage, *fallera*! We think it's so great to be a man, *fallera*!

MARIE It sounds as though you don't intend to go to work today.

PETER I'm not going until I get breakfast, anyway.

MARIE *(angry)* Peter!

PETER *(angry)* Marie!

SOFIE No, now I've heard enough. Good folks, how can you fight over such a minor matter?

MARIE A minor matter?

PETER A minor matter?

SOFIE Yes, a simple bagatelle. Listen, Marie, do you simply not want to grind coffee?

MARIE Not today at any rate.

SOFIE And you Peter, no chance?

PETER Nope!

SOFIE Well, then, I will. *(picks up the grinder)*

MARIE *(gets up, goes up to Sofie and grabs the grinder out of her hands)* No thank you, Sofie. It's none of your business to grind the coffee.

SOFIE But since neither you nor Peter want to—

MARIE He's grinding the coffee!

PETER *(to himself)* Women! These women! They are a difficult breed.

SOFIE Be reasonable, Marie. *(picks up the coffee grinder again)*

MARIE *(takes the grinder from her, again)* He's grinding the coffee.

PETER *(mimics Marie)* He's grinding the coffee. He's grinding the coffee. Yes, what do I do now? *(scratches his head)* If I give in, then I will have declared myself in favor of women's emancipation like the Americans. Then she'll become the man in the house and I will be left to be number zero! Hm! It's the fault of the Americans!

SOFIE It's almost seven o'clock, people. Isn't it time to think about breakfast?

PETER *(takes off his coat, his vest, and his boots, then lies down)*

MARIE What's this supposed to mean?

PETER Mean? It's not supposed to mean anything other than I'm going back to bed. Since I'm not going to work, I don't have anything else to do.

MARIE *(to herself)* Uff! Men! Men! They have to have their way in everything. Women are just unhappy beings, but just wait. Our time is coming. America will soon declare women free and equal to men. Then we'll be rid of all tyrants. *(looks at Peter)* Well, let him go back to bed. He seems to be determined in his decision. Hm! Maybe I should just give in? Well, maybe just this once. *(picks up the grinder, but sets it back down again)* No! I will not. I will not grind the coffee!

SOFIE Well, I better get to work, I can't afford to wait any longer.

MARIE You aren't leaving without having breakfast first?

SOFIE I have to. You don't want to grind the coffee, he doesn't want to grind the coffee, and I'm not allowed to grind the coffee.

MARIE But, don't you think I'm right?

SOFIE Oh, you know I don't want to get mixed up in your affairs.

MARIE But you have to stick with your own sex.

SOFIE Well, as far as that goes, you know I love the other sex more.

PETER Come here, Sofie, for that you deserve a kiss.

SOFIE Ha, ha, ha. *(motions towards Peter)*

MARIE *(pushes her away)* What kind of world are we living in? *(begins to cry)*

SOFIE But, my God, Marie, why are you crying? You have no reason to cry. Why must we make each other so unnecessarily miserable?

MARIE You talk like a goose! Just wait until you get married, then you will see things differently. *(cries)*

Scene 3: PETER, MARIE, SOFIE, FREDERIK

FREDERIK *(rushes in)* But Peter, aren't you going to work today? It's almost seven o'clock. But, what's happening here? You in bed looking as sour as a rat eating bad cheese. Your wife is crying. What's going on here? What is it? What is it?

PETER Oh, nothing!

FREDERIK Nothing? Don't give me that. Sofie, what's going on?

SOFIE Oh, nothing. It's just a bagatelle.

MARIE Just a bagatelle!

FREDERIK What is it, Sofie?

SOFIE Nothing more than Peter refuses to grind coffee.

FREDERIK Peter doesn't want to grind coffee? That's all?

SOFIE Yes, isn't it ridiculous?

FREDERIK Ha, ha, ha, now I really do have to laugh. Peter, you don't want to grind coffee?

PETER Nope!

FREDERIK And you too, Marie?

MARIE Nope!

FREDERIK Ha, ha, ha. All right, then I'll grind the coffee. *(grabs the grinder)*

SOFIE *(takes the grinder from him)* No, thank you. You are not grinding coffee!

FREDERIK Why not?

SOFIE Because you just aren't.

FREDERIK But that isn't a reason.

SOFIE It's reason enough.

FREDERIK *(grabs the grinder)* Nonsense, I'm going to grind some coffee.

SOFIE You are not!

FREDERIK I want to!

SOFIE You are not! *(takes the grinder)*

FREDERIK *(holds her away from him)* Stop this tomfoolery, Sofie. *(begins to grind the coffee)*

SOFIE *(tries to hinder him from grinding the coffee)* You are not to grind coffee!

FREDERIK But, why not?

SOFIE Because that's my job, not yours.

FREDERIK But, we aren't even married yet.

SOFIE No, but still— We will be married soon, but I want us to have the right relationship even *before* we're married.

MARIE Yes, just wait until you are married, then you'll be singing a different tune.

PETER Isn't that the truth?

FREDERIK No, this is complete foolishness. It doesn't matter who grinds the coffee.

PETER, MARIE, SOFIE Quite the contrary, it does matter!

FREDERIK Ah, you're being foolish, all three of you! Now, I'm grinding the coffee. *(grinds)*

SOFIE *(tries to take the grinder away from him)*

FREDERIK Stop it, Sofie, I mean it!

SOFIE *(still tries to take the grinder from him)*

FREDERIK Sofie, this is serious. Don't make me angry.

SOFIE I'm the one who is supposed to grind coffee, not you.

FREDERIK *(pushes against her. Continues to grind)*

SOFIE *(begins to cry)*

MARIE *(to Sofie)* There, you see what slaves women are. Are you going to be loyal to your sex now? Oh you tyrannical men! *(yells)*

PETER *(stands up, scatches his head, wrings his hands, walks back and forth on the stage)*

FREDERIK *(hums while he continues to grind the coffee)*

MARIE *(to Sofie)* Have your eyes finally been opened?

SOFIE Yes, terribly. I never would have thought Frederik could be so pigheaded! *(cries)*

MARIE Listen here, Sofie. Heed my advice, don't get married!

SOFIE Never! Never!

MARIE Will you now admit that I was right?

SOFIE Yes, you are right! It's true that marriage is slavery. I don't understand how any woman can endure marriage.

MARIE I can't endure it either.

SOFIE Listen, Marie. Divorce your husband. You're too good for him. He doesn't deserve you.

MARIE Yes, I will, this minute. Come on, Sofie, let's go!

SOFIE Yes, come on!

MARIE *(to Peter)* Good-bye you tyrant, you'll not see me again.

SOFIE *(to Frederik)* Farewell!

(they begin to go)

FREDERIK *(puts the grinder aside)* Sofie! Is it your intention to leave for good?

SOFIE Yes, you'll never see me again.

PETER *(has been standing with his arms crossed, staring at Marie)* Will you never return, Marie?

MARIE Never!

FREDERIK Well, Sofie, then I must thank you for the time we have had together. Farewell!

PETER Farewell, Marie!

(pause)

MARIE and SOFIE *(standing unsure at the door)*

PETER and FREDERIK *(casting glances at the door)*

SOFIE Did you say something, Frederik?

FREDERIK Me? No, I didn't say a word.

MARIE Don't you have any last words to say to me, Peter?

PETER Last words? No, not that I know of.

MARIE Well, then, farewell! You ungrateful— *(leaves with Sofie)*

PETER *(follows them)* Marie!

MARIE *(returns with Sofie)* Did you say something?

PETER Listen! I have a suggestion, a reasonable suggestion for all of us.

MARIE What suggestion?

PETER You, Marie, don't want to grind coffee, but Frederik will. I don't want to, but Sofie will. Well, it's pretty clear to me that Frederik is the one most appropriate for you and that Sofie and I fit best together. So, why not make an exchange? And I can get divorced, then you take Frederik and I take Sofie. That way you'll get a man willing to grind coffee. What do you say to my suggestion, good people?

MARIE Well, that doesn't sound too dumb.

PETER What do you say, Sofie?

SOFIE *(glances at Frederik)*

PETER What do you say, Frederik?

FREDERIK *(glances at Sofie)* Hm! I think that..., in a way, the suggestion is reasonable enough.

SOFIE *(to Frederik)* What? You think that's a reasonable suggestion? You mean you agree?

FREDERIK I didn't say that.

SOFIE So you don't agree?

FREDERIK I don't think so.

SOFIE So, you want to keep me?

FREDERIK I think that's probably the best.

SOFIE *(throws her arms around Frederik's neck)* Oh, you are my sweet Frederik. I knew you'd be true to me.

MARIE So, you want to divorce me, Peter?

PETER No, it seems to be you who no longer wants to live with me. What have you got against me? Have I been mean to you?

MARIE Mean? No...

PETER Then, why do you want to leave me?

MARIE Why? Because— because—

PETER Why?

MARIE Because you're unreasonable.

PETER Unreasonable? Don't I do almost everything you ask of me? Am I not as sensitive as a man can be? Answer me.

MARIE Yes, of course, but—

PETER Just because today I didn't want to grind coffee?

FREDERIK Listen, good people. We should all be ashamed. To sacrifice your relationship, Marie, on a minor bagatelle. Come here, give your husband your hand.

MARIE *(hesitates)*

FREDERIK Don't you want to give him your hand?

MARIE He can give me his hand.

FREDERIK *(to Peter)* Peter, give your wife your hand.

PETER *(looks at Marie)*

MARIE *(looks back at Peter)*

FREDERIK Now?

PETER and MARIE *(give each other their hands and hug each other)*

SOFIE *(applauds)*

FREDERIK Hurrah! Peace is declared!

MARIE No more fighting!

PETER No more fighting. Peace and harmony forever!

MARIE Yes, and now I want to grind some coffee.

PETER No, now I want to grind the coffee.

MARIE No, you are not allowed to.

PETER But I want to.

MARIE No, Peter, grinding coffee is my work.

PETER Yes, all right, but today I want to do it.

MARIE No, you are not allowed to.

SOFIE Tell me: Just a little while ago you were fighting because nobody wanted to grind coffee, but now you're fighting because both of you want to grind coffee. Well, neither of you are allowed to do it, because I'm going to grind the coffee.

FREDERIK You, Sofie?

SOFIE Yes, exactly, me! *(takes the coffee grinder)*

FREDERIK Don't I get to have any say in this matter?

SOFIE Oh, in God's name, go ahead and grind the coffee. Let's just quit arguing about this. *(gives Frederik the coffee grinder)*

PETER No, thank you, this isn't right. If any of us is going to grind the coffee, it'll be me. I'm the one who started this argument. *(takes the grinder from Frederik)*

MARIE No, Peter, it was my fault. *(takes the grinder from Peter)*

PETER *(takes the grinder from Marie)* No, Marie, it was not! Had I just ground the coffee when you asked me, this whole affair wouldn't have taken place.

MARIE *(takes back the grinder)* Peter, that's not right. I should have gotten up and ground the coffee and not asked you to do it.

FREDERIK The blame is really mine because it was none of my business to grind coffee when no one asked me to do it.

SOFIE The blame is really mine for being so dumb as to say he wasn't allowed to grind coffee.

ALL *(in each other's faces)* No, it's my fault. I was stubborn. I could have been more sensitive and therefore, it's my duty to grind the coffee.

PETER *(grabs the grinder from Frederik, Marie grabs it from Peter, Sofie takes it from Marie, then all four are grabbing for the grinder, pushing at each other. Finally, Frederik grabs it and...)*

FREDERIK Stop! *(holds the grinder high in the air)* I have a suggestion.

PETER What is it?

MARIE and SOFIE Let's hear it.

FREDERIK Since we can't agree on who's going to grind the coffee, I propose *nobody* grinds the coffee.

PETER But, then we won't get any coffee.

SOFIE We have to drink something warm before we go to work.

PETER Naturally, but we'll drink tea instead of coffee.

MARIE Tea? No thank you! Tea is much too tasteless a drink to have in the morning.

SOFIE I agree. It's clear we have to have coffee. *(grabs the grinder)*

FREDERICK, MARIE, PETER *(all grab for the grinder)*

SOFIE Listen here, good people! Now I have a suggestion: Since we must have coffee, and since we can't agree who's going to grind it, then let's agree that we all grind it at the same time.

PETER Now, that's a reasonable suggestion.

FREDERIK Sofie is clearly the most reasonable of us all. *(they put the table in the middle of the floor, put the grinder on the table)* So, everybody takes hold.

ALL *(holding the coffee grinder with their right hands)*

PETER All together, now. One... two... three...

ALL *(they grind the coffee while singing)*

CURTAIN FALLS

THE END

The Hypocrites

OR: LOVE DURING THE FIRE

A PLAY IN ONE ACT

FOR THE TOM PAINE CELEBRATION

Characters:

MR. FROM

MRS. FROM, his wife

CAROLINE, their daughter

MONSEN, Methodist minister and wheel maker

CHRISTIAN JENSEN

MIKKEL, hired hand

The play takes place during the Great Fire in Chicago, 1871.

Scene 1: FROM, MRS. FROM, CAROLINE

FROM *(is reading aloud from the Bible)*

MRS. FROM *(when From stops reading)* Amen! *(sighs)* That was beautiful! *(sighs even deeper)*

FROM *(closes the Bible, removes glasses from his nose)* Amen. *(he takes out his wallet)* I have to count my money. 100 – 200 – 300 – 400 – 500 – Yes, see here, I do have 500 dollars. I think I will offer Olsen 500 dollars. Then he'll sell me that lot.

MRS. FROM Yes, I should think so. He sits there with a big family and doesn't have enough to feed them. So, I would think he would be happy to get 500 dollars.

FROM I think so too. Just between us that lot is worth 1200 dollars; I know a man who is willing to pay 1200 dollars cash for it. If I can get it for 500, I will have gained 700, and 700 dollars is nothing to sneeze at.

CAROLINE But, dear father, since Olsen is so poor, isn't it proper that you let him know that there is a man willing to give 1200 dollars? Then that poor family would be in a better position.

MRS. FROM Be quiet! Don't stick your nose into business, that's something you just don't understand.

CAROLINE Yes, but it hurts me to see Olsen's family. Olsen is a hard-working and peaceful man. I feel sorry for him that he has to be so poor.

FROM Listen, my dear daughter, you talk like a simpleton. Olsen is poor because it is God's will that he remain humble until he comes to know the Truth. As long as he won't accept humility and become a member of the one True church, God cannot bless his work. And that would only strengthen him in his ungodly thoughts, and deeds. Look at me! I've become a rich man because I humble myself before God and do not neglect my daily prayers and meditations.

CAROLINE But Father, doesn't the Bible teach that a rich man can never come into the kingdom of heaven?*

FROM That Bible verse must be interpreted in the correct manner, my girl. It is the proud rich who despise the means of grace who cannot enter the kingdom of heaven. The humble rich, such as I, who pray and meditate day and night, are blessed by God and become even richer.

CAROLINE But doesn't it say that you are not to practice usury and that you are not to exploit the poor?

FROM But it is also written: He who has shall get and he who does not have, shall be taken from.** Therefore, it is God's will that I, who have, shall have more, but that Olsen, who does not have, shall have that lot he has taken from him.

CAROLINE Is this Christianity, Father?

FROM It is true Christianity when the scriptures are interpreted in the correct manner.

CAROLINE I don't understand that kind of Christianity.

FROM No, Caroline, you don't understand the understanding because you do not have the Spirit. You are too much of a child of this world, Caroline, and children of this world cannot understand those things which belong to God's Spirit.

---

*See Matthew 19:23–24.

**See Matthew 13:12; 25:29; Mark 4:24–25; Luke 8:18; 19:26.

CAROLINE But, I don't understand—

MRS. FROM Be quiet, you dumb girl, and stop this scandalous talk. Go down to the kitchen and wash the cups.

CAROLINE *(exits to the left)*

Scene 2: FROM and MRS. FROM

MRS. FROM *(sighs)* Oh, dear God! Caroline is so possessed by the spirit of this world that there is danger for her soul.

FROM Yes, yes, yes! The spirit of this world! *(sighs)*

MRS. FROM As soon as we can, we must get her married.

FROM Get her married! Yes, of course, that would be the best, but with whom?

MRS. FROM Naturally, with Pastor Monsen.

FROM With the wheel maker, you mean?

MRS. FROM Yes, of course, the wheel maker. Our pastor.

FROM Yes, yes. He is a man of God and we could not hope to see our daughter in better hands—as far as the spiritual is concerned. But, you know, my dear wife, that there is also the temporal to consider and Monsen is a man with no fortune.

MRS. FROM Monsen is a man without a fortune, you say? No, you are wrong. Monsen is a richer man than anyone thinks.

FROM That is not possible.

MRS. FROM Oh yes, it's true. But he is a careful man. He doesn't let anyone know what he really has. After all, didn't he make a great *coup* here a couple of years ago?

FROM A *coup*? What *coup*?

MRS. FROM He traveled around up in Wisconsin collecting contributions for a new church building—

FROM Yes, but—

MRS. FROM You don't know how much money he took in, especially from the Yankees. He got at least $6,000, and you know, just between us, that the church he built couldn't have cost more than $2,000. Oh yes, he certainly made about $4,000 on that deal.

FROM Is that really true?

MRS. FROM As true as I am sitting here, a sinner in the eyes of God.

FROM Well, that makes me very happy for him. If it is true then we need have no reservations about letting him have our daughter. But, how do you know this?

MRS. FROM Well, you remember last year when you traveled around in Illinois and Iowa in order to raise money for the needy in Sweden, and you came home with $2,000—

FROM *(interrupting)* Yes, yes, yes, let's talk about something else. Ahh, let me see, I had— $500 *(looks for his wallet)* yes, that's right, $500. *(replaces his wallet)* Jesus!

MRS. FROM Jesus!

FROM I think it best that we go to bed. *(looks at his watch)* The time is already 11:30 and Monsen isn't coming as he had promised.

MRS. FROM Is it already 11:30? Yes, I think we better go to bed. It won't do any good to stay up any longer waiting for Monsen. It doesn't look like he's coming.

Scene 3: FROM, MRS. FROM, MIKKEL, CAROLINE

MIKKEL *(charges in)* There's a big fire on the West Side.

MRS. FROM *(clasping her hands together)* Oh, another fire has been started. I mean, one of these days they'll burn the entire city.

MIKKEL No, this one wasn't started on purpose. They say a cow kicked over a kerosene lamp in a barn.

MRS. FROM Nonsense, it was deliberately set. We had a fire last night and now tonight, another? Of course it's deliberate.

MIKKEL But, who would be starting fires in the city?

MRS. FROM Who else but the Freethinkers? Those children of the Devil.

MIKKEL Yes, that's true. It must be the Freethinkers. Ooh, ooh, those Freethinkers. They are some kind of terrible people. Ooh! Ooh!

FROM You said it was on the West Side?

MIKKEL Yes.

FROM Yes, well, then there is no danger to my property. So we might as well just go to bed.

CAROLINE *(enters)* My God! I think there is another fire tonight. The whole sky is red. *(to Mikkel)* Where did you say it was?

MIKKEL On the West Side.

CAROLINE Yes, but where?

MIKKEL It must be around 12th Street, or around there—

CAROLINE My God! Then Mrs. Petersen is in danger. Come, Father, we have to hurry if we are going to be able to help save—

FROM Nonsense. Do you think I'm going such a long way in the middle of the night? No, come on, let's just go to bed.

CAROLINE Are you really just going to go to bed now?

FROM Of course I am. There is no danger for us. Come along now, Mother.

MRS. FROM That's right, the best we can do is just go to bed.

(From and Mrs. From exit to the left)

CAROLINE Mikkel! Come with me over to 12th Street.

MIKKEL No, I don't want to, and Mr. From wouldn't like it if I left the house now.

CAROLINE Well then, at least you can run over to the police station and let somebody know where the fire is.

MIKKEL Yes, Ma'am. I will do *dat! (he runs out the back door)*

CAROLINE I have to get out there. That poor Mrs. Petersen with four little children! What if her house is burning! I'll get dressed. *(runs out to the left)*

Scene 4: JENSEN, CAROLINE, MIKKEL

JENSEN *(enters from rear)* I'm not sure the old folks have gone to bed.

(walks carefully forward) Oh yes, they've gone to bed. *(listens)* Somebody's coming!

(he runs to the back door, but when he sees it is Caroline, he walks forward again)

CAROLINE *(enters wearing a shawl and hat)*

JENSEN Oh! My darling Caroline, I get a chance to talk with you this evening, that is more than I had expected.

CAROLINE Come, Christian. Come with me down to 12th Street. I think Mrs. Petersen is caught in the fire.

JENSEN No, you can relax. I've just come from the fire and the wind is blowing from the south, so Mrs. Petersen is in no danger.

CAROLINE Thank God! I was so worried about her.

JENSEN Come here, Caroline. Let me give you a hug. I have missed you so much.

CAROLINE Leave me alone, Christian. It does no good that we see each other more often. We can never have each other.

JENSEN Not have each other? Oh yes, my dear Caroline, even if all the devils of this world conspire against me, you shall be mine.

CAROLINE That is easy for you to say. But, all in all, it is not that easy.

JENSEN But it must be easy. Love conquers all.

CAROLINE Oh, you don't know everything. And you don't know my parents. They will never agree that I shall be your wife.

JENSEN Why not?

CAROLINE Oh, for many reasons.

JENSEN Name me one.

CAROLINE In the first place, you are poor.

JENSEN Poor? Yes, I'm poor now, but I can work. I'm a good lumberman.

CAROLINE Yes, that may be enough for you and me, but it is not enough for my parents.

JENSEN And what are the other reasons?

CAROLINE Because you do not have the right religion.

JENSEN The right religion? Why, I don't have any religion.

CAROLINE Shame on you, Christian. Don't talk like that. Of course you have a religion.

JENSEN Well, my whole religion consists of being an honorable and decent person—if you can call that religion. I say with Thomas Paine: "The world is my Fatherland and my religion is to do good."

CAROLINE Oh, let's not debate religion, you know that we don't agree. But my parents are of the opinion that anyone who is not a Methodist is of the Devil. And you know that they will not give their daughter to a devil.

JENSEN To a devil, no! I would not do that either if I had a daughter. But do you really believe that everyone who is not a Methodist is of the Devil?

CAROLINE Naturally, Don't you know that?

JENSEN No, I didn't think you were totally crazy— no, I'm sorry, I don't mean totally crazy, I mean unreasonable.

CAROLINE Oh, my God! Religion, religion. That it should cause enmity between people instead of bringing them together in love.

JENSEN But, then what are we going to do, Caroline?

CAROLINE Hush, here comes Mikkel. Don't let him see you.

JENSEN *(hides behind the curtains)*

MIKKEL *(enters)* Did you say something, Caroline? Ooh.

CAROLINE Say something?

MIKKEL Ooh! Ooh!

CAROLINE What are you doing?

MIKKEL I thought I saw somebody here a minute ago.

CAROLINE Somebody? Who could that be?

MIKKEL That's what I'd like to know. I saw somebody sneak into the alley, over by the stable. I didn't see if he went upstairs or downstairs, but I am sure it was somebody. Ooh, ooh, I am so scared that—

CAROLINE What are you afraid of?

MIKKEL Oh, what if it was a Freethinker. He could kill us, everybody. Or set fire to the house.

CAROLINE Oh, that's ridiculous!

MIKKEL Ridiculous? No it is not. It was the Freethinkers who set the fire yesterday and now they have set a fire again. *(suddenly startled)* What was that? Ooh! I think I just heard something! The Freethinkers are definitely close by here! Ooh! He'll kill me, sure enough, he'll kill me. I'm going in to wake Mr. From. *(runs out to the left)*

JENSEN *(comes forward)* I do believe he is crazy.

CAROLINE Go, Christian. You have to understand that this house is not for you and that we can never have each other. We must not think of each other, that is the best for us both.

JENSEN Is that your love, Caroline? Can you give me up so easily? Oh, I understand. You have found someone else. Someone who has money. Money first and money last—uff! What a damned world of money we live in. Yes, yes, Caroline, since the money devil has possessed you, we better end it. *(starts to go)*

CAROLINE No, no, Christian, you are going to leave me like that? Shame on you! Do I deserve to be treated like this by you?

JENSEN No, no. Forgive me. But what are we going to do? Will you run away with me?

CAROLINE What are you saying? Run away with you?

JENSEN Of course.

CAROLINE But that would be a sin.

JENSEN Doesn't it say in the scriptures that a woman shall leave her father and mother and follow her husband?*

CAROLINE Is that in the scriptures?

JENSEN Of course it is. Don't you know the scriptures?

CAROLINE Show me where it is written.

---

*See Genesis 2:24; Matthew 19:5.

JENSEN *(looks it up in a Bible)*

Scene 5: JENSEN, CAROLINE, MIKKEL, FROM, MRS. FROM

MIKKEL *(enters)* I tell you, there must be a Freethinker in the house. *(whispers)* So this is not the time to sleep.

MRS. FROM *(whispering)* A Freethinker in our house!

FROM *(whispering)* A Freethinker, that's impossible.

JENSEN *(reading aloud)* "Therefore shall a wife leave her father and mother and follow her husband."

MRS. FROM But, what is this? Caroline with a young man! Caroline!

CAROLINE *(gives a shriek of surprise)*

JENSEN *(stands and bows)*

MRS. FROM *(takes Caroline aside)* Who is this young man?

CAROLINE *(disoriented)* Ah, ah— it is Mr. Jensen.

FROM What is going on here?

CAROLINE Ah, ah— We were reading the Bible.

MRS. FROM Really? You are reading the Bible? That's very nice.

FROM When you come here to read the Bible with my daughter, young man, you are most welcome in my house. It is not often that young people these days have a sense for spiritual matters. I welcome you to my house.

JENSEN Thank you very much.

MRS. FROM Welcome to our house!

JENSEN Thank you very much.

MIKKEL *(looking carefully at Jensen)* Aren't you a Freethinker?

FROM Do you know my daughter?

JENSEN Yes, thank you very much.

MRS. FROM Our daughter is unfortunately not as religious as we would have liked. That is why we appreciate seeing someone reading the scripture with her, that is to say when it is presented in the right way.

FROM You are a Methodist, I take it?

JENSEN A Methodist? Ah— yes. I have my methods and...am...naturally a methodist.

FROM Yes, yes, naturally, it depends on the method of interpretation. Are you a schoolteacher?

JENSEN No, I follow the Apostle Paul's example and work with my two strong arms.

MRS. FROM Yes, Paul's example can be a very good one, but that was from his own time. The world has changed much since then and has more temporal needs!

FROM Well, we won't disturb you further. You can stay; we will go back to bed.

JENSEN *(to himself)* Well, it is now or never. *(to Mr. From)* Mr. From, you must excuse me, but—

FROM Oh, no, don't apologize.

JENSEN Yes, as a matter of fact, I have something important that I must speak with you about.

FROM Oh? Something about the fire?

JENSEN No, no. You see— Ah— As a matter of fact— You know that it is written that it is "not good for man to be alone."*

FROM Yes, that is sensible.

JENSEN And it is not good for me, either. I am thinking about getting married. I have spoken with your daughter about it and she has said yes—so all that remains is to have your permission.

FROM But—

MRS. FROM But— *(to Caroline)* You have gone and promised yourself without us knowing about it, have you?

CAROLINE *(silent)*

FROM My young friend, we do not know you. This is a very important matter. Do you have any money?

---

*See Genesis 2:18.

MIKKEL I am sure that he is a Freethinker!

FROM Well, my dear friend, this matter requires some serious consideration.

Scene 6: JENSEN, CAROLINE, MIKKEL, FROM, MRS. FROM, MONSEN

MONSEN *(enters)*

MIKKEL *(startled)* Ooh! Who is that? Oh, it's Mr. Monsen. I thought it was a Freethinker. Uff. I don't want to stay inside. *(runs out)*

MONSEN *(gravely)* Good afternoon, friends in Christ. Tonight God's judgment is being visited on many of the ungodly.

MRS. FROM So true! *(sighs)*

FROM Have you been bothered by the fire, my brother?

MONSEN Clearly and truly, but that matter has nothing to do with us. We need not worry. God always looks after his own.

MRS. FROM Those are beautiful words. *(sighs)*

FROM My brother! Allow me to introduce you to a young man, a fellow brother in Christ. *(introduces Jensen to Monsen)*

MONSEN *(places his glasses on, examines Jensen from head to toe)* God save this house, Brother From!

FROM What do you mean, Brother Monsen?

MONSEN God's children must not let the ungodly cross the threshold of their house!

MRS. FROM What do you mean?

FROM Do you know him? What do you know about him?

MONSEN *(slowly)* He has the Devil in him.

FROM and MRS. FROM *(clapping their hands)* Oh! He has the Devil in him?

MRS. FROM But, what do you know about him?

MONSEN *(slowly)* He is a *Freethinker*!

FROM *(claps his hands together)* A Freethinker! Holy Sabbath!

MRS. FROM *(throws herself on a chair)* Oh dear peaceable God! A Freethinker! In our house! A Freethinker who has proposed to our daughter!

FROM *(to Jensen)* Young man! Is this true, are you a Freethinker?

JENSEN Yes, ah— what do you mean by a "Freethinker"? Do you mean someone who thinks freely?

FROM I mean one who does not believe in the Bible as the revealed Word of God.

JENSEN Well, I don't want to stand here as a hypocrite or liar. I must admit, I am a Freethinker.

MRS. FROM Oh, a Freethinker! Get him out, get him out!

FROM This is terrible!

MONSEN *(to Mrs. From)* Get him out of the house. As soon as possible.

MRS. FROM *(to From)* Throw him out, I said. Throw him out so he can no longer contaminate our holy house.

FROM *(makes a motion to throw Jensen out)*

JENSEN Oh, don't do anything special on my account, Mr. From. It will not be necessary to throw me out. I will leave willingly. Farewell, Caroline. *(reaches out his hand)*

MRS. FROM *(screams)* Don't touch that ungodly hand, Caroline. Oh, God. To think that my daughter has been together with a Freethinker!

JENSEN Farewell, we will see you again. *(he leaves)*

MIKKEL *(as Jensen is leaving, Mikkel enters, follows Jensen, taunting him and pointing his finger at him. He spits at him and kicks the air after him)*

Scene 7: CAROLINE, MIKKEL, FROM, MRS. FROM, MONSEN

FROM Thank God, we have gotten rid of him.

MRS. FROM But why did you let him take Caroline's hand?

FROM Ah, how could I have prevented that?

MRS. FROM Of course you could have.

FROM I could not have.

MRS. FROM Yes, you could have.

FROM No, I said, I could not.

MRS. FROM Yes, I say.

FROM Will you now shut up!

MRS. FROM Shut up? No, I will not shut up. Why have you not watched Caroline so she would not meet someone so ungodly?

FROM Shut up! *(threatening)*

MRS. FROM Perhaps you want to beat me again just as you did last week?

FROM Yes, when a wife refuses to obey her husband as the scriptures require, and good words don't help, then a man must use his power. It is written that the man shall have power over woman.* Isn't that true, Brother Monsen?

MONSEN Wise and true!

MRS. FROM But think! A Freethinker in our holy house! Oh! It is a bad omen for us all, and it is *your* fault!

FROM *(cuffs Mrs. From on the ear)* Will you now shut up?

MRS. FROM It is your fault, I say.

FROM *(hits her again and pulls her hair)*

MRS. FROM Ow! Ow! Let me go! I will shut up, just don't hit me again.

FROM *(stops)* Now, have you learned to shut up? Have you learned your duty as a Christian housewife?

MRS. FROM Yes, yes, but—

FROM Not a syllable more—do you hear? *(threatening)*

MRS. FROM *(covers her mouth with both hands)*

---

*See Ephesians 5:21–23.

FROM There, Brother Monsen. Now we have a Christian peace just as it should be in a Christian home.

MONSEN Amen!

FROM *(to Mrs. From)* Go to bed now, Wife, and remember the Christian reprimand I have given you.

MRS. FROM Can't I have permission to sit here if I don't say a word?

FROM Yes, you can, but not a single word! Remember that.

MONSEN In truth, you can praise God that you got that young man out of this house. That he is a Freethinker is the least of it.

FROM What are you saying, Brother? Can there be anything worse than being a Freethinker?

MONSEN Yes, there is something much worse. Even among the children of the Devil there are levels of evil. And he is one of the worst. Imagine that he is— I am almost afraid to say the word—

FROM What is he? What is he?

MONSEN *(slowly)* He is— is— an International!*

MRS. FROM *(screams and falls on the floor)* International! International!

FROM *(wrings his hands)* An International! *(lifts Mrs. From up from the floor)*

MRS. FROM An assassin of kings!

FROM A pyromaniac!

MRS. FROM We are all lost! Our house is condemned.

FROM Oh, despair!

MRS. FROM And it is *your* fault. Why haven't you, as a man—

FROM Are you starting again?

---

*The International Workingman's Association (First International) was founded in 1864 in the wake of the failed European revolutions of 1848. Its supporters were considered to be extreme political radicals with socialist and anarchist sympathies. The International advocated workers' rights, an 8-hour day, antimilitarism, and anticapitalism, all ideals generally supported by Thrane himself.

MRS. FROM Yes, why haven't you as a m— prevented—

FROM *(pulls her hair and hits her)* Get out. *(pushes her out of the room)*

Scene 8: FROM and MONSEN

FROM Well, my dear Brother Monsen, we have to accept the fate of Providence. This was a difficult test and probably punishment for our sins.

MONSEN Wisely so!

FROM The next time you give a sermon in the church, I hope you will pray for our house, that the Lord will protect it.

MONSEN Truly.

FROM But, we better also think about our business affairs.

MONSEN Yes, that is the purpose of my coming here.

FROM Have you gotten much money in for the mission?

MONSEN No, my brother in Christ, not much money. You know how ungodly the world is these days.

FROM *(squinting at him)* So, you haven't got much money collected?

MONSEN No, my brother, not much more than $150.

FROM *(squinting)* Not more than $150? How is that possible, my brother in Christ? I thought you would at least have gotten $600, and I saw myself at the last meeting that you collected over $200.

MONSEN But, my brother, you know there are always expenses.

FROM Naturally, but in the last two meetings, more money was also collected.

MONSEN Well, one brother can't be too critical of the other. We have to excuse each other and recognize that we mean the best, as the scriptures say. I did that a few months ago when you collected money for that new church.

FROM *(looking around)* Yes, yes, my brother. Let's not speak anymore of that. It is as you say. We need to believe and speak well of one another. Everything is meant to be for the best. It is important that we avoid cause for offense.

MONSEN Exactly! That is what is important. But, tell me, Brother, regarding Caroline, it would be good if there could be a final decision.

FROM Yes, yes. The matter is decided. You will have my daughter. I could wish her in no better hands. But now I am thirsty, what do you say to a glass of lemonade?

MONSEN That would taste good right now.

FROM *(shouts)* Caroline! Caroline!

Scene 9: FROM, MONSEN, CAROLINE, MIKKEL

CAROLINE *(enters)* Do you want something, Father?

FROM Bring us two glasses of lemonade!

CAROLINE *(leaves, and returns shortly with two glasses of lemonade)*

MIKKEL *(enters)* Mr. From, there is a message from Mr. Halvorsen if he can borrow the horse and wagon in order to move a load. He's afraid he'll lose his things in the fire and he can't get a horse and wagon under $40, he says.

FROM Forty dollars for a load! Well, I don't want to let him use it for nothing.

CAROLINE But, Father, you aren't going to take money from Halvorsen to move a couple of loads for him?

FROM Be quiet, daughter. *(to Mikkel)* Tell the messenger that I will let him have the horse and wagon for $20 a load.

MIKKEL *(leaves)*

FROM *(to Caroline)* Is the lemonade strong or weak?

CAROLINE It is weak, but here is the cognac, which you can add as you wish.

FROM Help yourself, Brother Monsen.

MONSEN Thank you, Brother. That will taste good. After all, Paul says in his second letter to the Corinthians that a little wine is good for the stomach.*

---

*See I Timothy 5:23.

FROM Truly. But just to make sure that no one will be bothered by it, I will close the door.

MONSEN So true, Brother.

FROM Caroline! Close the door when you go.

CAROLINE *(closes the door and leaves)*

FROM Cheers, Brother!

MONSEN Cheers, Brother!

FROM There was one thing I wanted to ask your advice on. You are the Lord's servant and know how to express yourself correctly.

MONSEN What is on your heart, my brother?

FROM Well, you see. Regarding money and the value of money—it is my opinion that they come into the hands of God's children, rather than that they remain in the hands of the ungodly.

MONSEN Truly! The ungodly use their money for vanity and nonsense and all sorts of ungodly things. God's children, on the other hand, use it in the honor of God and for the benefit of their neighbor.

FROM You speak like a wise man.

MONSEN It is clearly written that we are to befriend the unrighteous mammon.*

FROM Exactly. You see, in this case, I loaned Grocer Johnson $200 a couple of years ago. This spring, while I was away, he came and delivered the $200 to my wife, and got no receipt. There were also no witnesses that he gave the money to my wife. What do you think of this?

MONSEN Yes, and you know what, my brother. Scripture teaches us clearly that we are to be friends with the unrighteous mammon. In the parable about the unfaithful servant, you remember how the servant allowed his master's debtors to pay 50 barrels of oil instead of 100.** My opinion is that you should do the same.

FROM That is also my opinion. Cheers!

MONSEN Tell me, Brother. Do you have much of your fortune in real estate?

---

*See Luke 16:9.

**See Luke 16:5–6.

FROM Yes, most of it, don't you as well? Why do you ask?

MONSEN Yes, you see, I'm thinking about the fire. I am a little uncomfortable. Here on the North Side, of course, there is naturally no danger, but it is possible to conceive of the South Side being attacked.

FROM Oh, far from it. It's impossible. We have a very capable fire department and plenty of hydrants. Oh no, we can take it easy.

Scene 10: CAROLINE, MIKKEL, FROM, MRS. FROM, MONSEN

MIKKEL *(knocks from the outside)*

FROM Somebody's coming. *(puts the glasses and the bottle under the table)*

MIKKEL *(knocks louder)* Open up!

FROM What is it? What is it? *(opens the door)*

MIKKEL Ah! God save us altogether! The whole city is full of Commulister [sic] and Freethinkers who are setting fire to the city. Now the whole South Side is burning.

FROM Are you crazy? The South Side burning?

MONSEN Oh! Poor me, most of my property is on the South Side.

FROM It hasn't reached Monroe Street yet?

MIKKEL Oh, all of Monroe went a long time ago. And Court. The house has burned and everything. And no insurance companies are paying anymore.

FROM *(sinks to his knees)* Now, I am the most unfortunate man in the world.

MONSEN I have to go see if there is anything I can save. *(he leaves)*

FROM Caroline! Mother! Mother! Caroline!

MRS. FROM and CAROLINE *(enter)* What is it?

FROM We are lost. We have lost everything.

MRS. FROM What is it now?

FROM We are beggars. The whole South Side is burning and my office has burned up. My bonds, my documents, protocols, my cash. All gone. We have become beggars.

MRS. FROM *(faints)*

MIKKEL Yes, and even more, it is the Freethinkers and the Commulists who have set fire to the city and they say they will not leave a single house in the city standing.

MRS. FROM *(had come to during Mikkel's speech and, upon hearing it, faints again with a scream)*

MIKKEL And think! The whole city is full of robbers who are plundering houses and killing people and these robbers call themselves Internationalists!

FROM Lock the door, Mikkel! Close the door securely. Imagine if Internationalists come here!

MIKKEL *(closes the door) (shortly thereafter, an explosion is heard)*

FROM *(falls to his knees)*

MRS. FROM *(screams)*

MIKKEL *(under the table, but still visible to the audience. Finding the bottle, he takes a drink now and then)*

Scene 11: CAROLINE, MIKKEL, FROM, MRS. FROM, JENSEN

JENSEN *(outside banging loudly on the door)*

MIKKEL Ooh! Here come the Internationalists. Ooh! (*takes a drink*)

FROM and MRS. FROM *(fearful)* What is it?

JENSEN *(banging)*

FROM Who is it? Who is it?

JENSEN It's me.

FROM Who, me?

CAROLINE *(enters)* What is going on here?

FROM There is someone who is trying to get in.

CAROLINE So, let's open up then. *(goes to open the door)*

MIKKEL For God's sake, don't open the door. It's the Commulists and the Freethinkers coming to kill us all.

CAROLINE Oh, nonsense!

JENSEN Open up! Open up!

FROM Who is it?

JENSEN Christian Jensen.

CAROLINE Oh, is it you, Christian? *(she opens)*

FROM, MRS. FROM, and MIKKEL *(all try to keep her from opening, but too late) (they pull at each other's shirts trying to be first)*

JENSEN *(enters carrying papers and protocols)*

MRS. FROM Oh, God! It's the Freethinker again! Get him out! Get him out! He will only bring bad luck down on all of us. Mikkel! Run and get a policeman!

MIKKEL I'm too scared to move. He'll kill me!

FROM Get out of this house, you ungodly person!

MRS. FROM Get out, you arsonist!

JENSEN I will go as soon as I finish what I came here for. Here are your protocols, Mr. From, including papers and much more.

FROM My protocols? How? My protocols and papers were saved?

JENSEN Yes, here they are.

FROM But, how could that be? My office has burned to the ground!

JENSEN When I saw that the fire had reached the building where you had your office, I kicked in the door and smashed your safe and picked up what I could carry and brought it here to you. I had to leave some books since it had already begun to burn in the office.

FROM You saved my money, too?

JENSEN Your money? Well, you see, with money it's no big deal in this world.

FROM I said, do you have my money?

JENSEN I don't know, I always walk around with $5000 in my pockets.

FROM Give it to me.

JENSEN Oh, no. Don't be in such a big hurry.

FROM Give me my money, I say, or I will send for the police.

MIKKEL Yes, get the police.

JENSEN Ha, ha, ha. Well. Since you want to call the police, I guess it's best that I get out of here. The police worry me. *(begins to go)*

FROM No, no, no— stay, stay, stay. I will not send for the police, but let me have my money.

JENSEN I said I had $5000 in my pocket, but I did not say it was *your* money.

FROM But, since you have taken my protocols from my safe, you have also taken my money.

JENSEN That has not been said. At any rate, you cannot *prove* that the money I have in my pocket is *your* money. It could be that I let your money burn and I saved this money from somebody else's safe.

FROM Yes, that is true, I have to accept that. Now look here, young man, you look too honest to be willing to make a whole family unhappy.

JENSEN That depends.

FROM You don't want to reduce us to begging?

JENSEN Oh, who knows?

MRS. FROM Caroline. *You* talk to him!

CAROLINE Dear Christian! Don't be hard-hearted.

JENSEN Hard-hearted? Is it I who is hard-hearted?

FROM *(to himself)* Well, in God's name. *(he takes Caroline's and Jensen's hands and joins them)* I understand what you want, young man. Here is the hand of my daughter.

JENSEN *(takes the money from his pocket and gives it to From)*

MIKKEL *(has crawled out from under the table)* Is Caroline going to get a Freethinker? That beats all that I have ever heard.

MRS. FROM But, my dear husband, you are going to give our only daughter to a Freethinker?

FROM Well, a Freethinker isn't really such a dangerous person as you may think in your naiveté. In reality, when push comes to shove, we are all Freethinkers. In the very least, we have been shown that Jensen is an honest and honorable young man.

MRS. FROM But he is also an Internationalist.

MIKKEL Doesn't that beat it all?

MRS. FROM He's one of those who set fire to Chicago.

FROM That's nonsense. Do you really think that he would first set fire to our house and then risk his life to save our money?

MRS. FROM No, that's probably true enough. But, imagine, an Internationalist Freethinker for a son-in-law.

JENSEN Well, my honorable mother-in-law, don't be too worried about getting a Freethinker as a relative. Just remember what the scripture says, that you are to go among the publicans and the sinners.* If I am a great sinner, then you're acting especially Christian-like to have anything to do with me. Who knows, maybe you'll even convert me one day.

MRS. FROM Yes, imagine that. That I could convert you to see the Light.

FROM *(to himself)* Convert a Freethinker? That won't be in this lifetime.

MIKKEL I bet you a dollar!

JENSEN But, Caroline, would you actually have an ungodly man such as I?

CAROLINE I look only at the character of my man. If that is good, then, in my eyes, he has a good religion.

JENSEN Well, then let us all live in accordance with Thomas Paine's religion: "The World is my Fatherland, and my religion is to do good."

CURTAIN FALLS

THE END

*See Luke 15:1–2; 16:9.

Holden

(OR: BE PATIENT!)

A SYNOD OPERA IN THREE ACTS

Characters:

BERNT, Synod minister
MRS. BERNT, his wife
JOHNNY, son (6 years old)
KARN, servant girl (deaf and dumb)
SCHWEINIGEL, saloon keeper
KÄTCHEN, his daughter
OLA NAUTEBY
MR. PRESS, reporter
MRS. OLSEN
MR. HANSEN
BOYS A, B, C, D
GIRLS A, B, C, D
MR. GALGEBERG, farmer

Synod ministers:
OLE TOSKEBERG
HALVOR ASENBY
PETER RÆVELAND
SÖREN FAARELUND

Congregation Members

Act 1

Open square. To the left, a meeting house. To the right, a saloon.

Scene 1: MR. PRESS

PRESS *(well dressed, cane, portfolio under his arm, enters from right, looks around)* Being a reporter is surely a funny occupation. In order to succeed, one has to hunt for huge sensations, visit palaces and huts, stand face to face with robbers and thieves. In short, a reporter must stick his nose into everything. I should know, I'm a reporter from St. Paul. Ah, but never mind. I cannot deny that the life is interesting. His eye must be keen and his pen sharp. We uncover whatever happens in this society, from north to south and all around. A reporter must put his nose into everything. I certainly do, this reporter from St. Paul.

Scene 2: Mr. Press, Ola Nauteby

(Ola Nauteby enters)

Press Hello! Glad to see somebody. Say! I understand that the Norwegians are going to have a meeting here today? Is that so?

Ola *(looks at him, without speaking)*

Press The Norwegians are going to have a meeting here today? Isn't that so?

Ola *(looks at him and shakes his head)*

Press Don't you understand what I am saying?

Ola *(shakes his head)*

Press Can you speak?

Ola Speak? Of course I can speak.

Press Can you speak English?

Ola English, no, I can't speak English; I can only speak Norwegian.

Press Oh, have you just recently arrived from the old country?

Ola You mean from Norway?

Press Yes, from Norway.

Ola I've never been to Norway.

Press Where have you been then?

Ola I've never been outside of Goodhue County, right here in Minnesota.

Press What? You're born here in America and you've been here all your life, and still you can't speak English?

Ola No, and where the devil should I have learned English?

Press But, my dear friend, didn't you learn English in the public school?

Ola What did you say? You better speak Norwegian.

Press I said, didn't you learn English in school?

Ola No, they only taught in Norwegian there.

Press Oh! You only studied Norwegian? Did you never go to English school?

OLA What did you say?

PRESS I said, have you never gone to the English school—the common school?*

OLA The common school, are you kidding?

PRESS Never went to a common school? Why not?

OLA The minister wouldn't allow us to attend the common school.

PRESS What? Is your minister crazy? Crazy in the head maybe?

OLA *Our* minister crazy? I think you are crazy for saying such a thing. Our minister is the best minister in the whole country of America—and everything he teaches and says is right, whether it is right or not. He only teaches that which is true and right, because he has his teachings from God himself, so they must be right.

PRESS And the minister forbids you to attend the English school?

OLA Yes, and for that he deserves thanks, because there are only children of the Devil at the common school, and it's dangerous to have anything to do with them. You Americans, you're so ungodly, besides, you don't care what happens to your soul after death, but we Norwegians aren't like that. At least those of us who belong to the Synod. God knows that even among us Norwegians there are many who've gone astray. We have among us Methodists and Baptists and Frankeans and Ellingians, and many who belong to the Conference. Yes! those who belong to the Conference are lost for sure.**

---

*Critics of the public schools, the so-called "common school," ministers of the Norwegian Synod advocated religious schools for the children of the denomination. For a brief introduction to this topic, see Theodore C. Blegen, "The Immigrant and the Common School," in *The Norwegian Migration to America: The American Transition* (Northfield, MN, 1940) 241–276.

**Thrane refers here to various Norwegian-American Lutheran denominations and their controversies. The Norwegian-Danish Conference (1870) included many congregations with a pietistic orientation. The Norwegian Synod (1853) espoused a theology like that of the German-American Missouri Synod and was served by a considerable number of ministers educated in Norway. "Ellingians" were members of a strenuously pietistic body, the Eielsen Synod (1846) founded by the Norwegian revivalist Elling Eielsen (1804–1883). "Frankeans" refers to a German-American body, the Frankean Synod (1837), with which some dissident Ellingians for a time associated. The comment by Ola is likely a reference to controversies in the Norwegian Synod over predestination and conversion that led to the departure of a number of congregations from the Synod and eventually to their affiliation with the United Norwegian Lutheran Church in America (1890).

PRESS Ha, ha, ha, ha.

OLA What are you laughing at?

PRESS Ha, ha, ha, ha. Oh! Excuse me, I can't help it. Ha, ha.

OLA What the devil are you laughing—

PRESS The devil, you say? Aren't you afraid to curse?

OLA Oh, no! Cursing is not dangerous.

PRESS Cursing isn't dangerous? What about lying then? Is lying not dangerous?

OLA Lying? No, that can't be so dangerous.

PRESS But, what then is dangerous?

OLA There is only one thing that's dangerous.

PRESS And what is that?

OLA That is to not believe—not to have the true faith—and no one can get the true faith without being in the Synod. If one has the true faith, it doesn't matter much what one does, because it is only with the true faith that one can be saved.

PRESS *(aside, to himself)* Am I really living in the nineteenth century? *(pinches himself)* Am I awake, or am I dreaming?

OLA Did you say something? If you want to talk to me, you have to speak Norwegian.

PRESS *(to himself)* Well, perhaps this boy will be able to give me some information regarding the minister and his wife. *(loudly)* Say! Say, have you heard that your minister has been very mean to his wife?

OLA Mean to his wife? What kind of talk is that? He has to teach his wife to respect the Fourth Commandment, doesn't he? Or maybe you think that we Norwegians want our womenfolk to be like the Americans and not respect the Fourth Commandment? No thank you! The wife must submit to her husband, and even if the husband is very strict, the woman has to accept that. Otherwise, she sins against the Fourth Commandment and God help her soul when she dies.

PRESS So, the Fourth Commandment is a very important commandment?

OLA The Fourth Commandment is the most important of all commandments, because it has to do with obedience and submissiveness.

PRESS But, what about the Seventh Commandment, isn't that an important commandment?

OLA Oh, it isn't as important if one truly has the belief.

PRESS Oh, so you would say that it is alright that your minister has taken $4000 from his wife?

OLA Oh, what gossip! Everything a wife has belongs to her husband. A wife has no right to anything. She has to keep the Fourth Commandment.

PRESS But, what about the Sixth Commandment?

OLA What did you say? You have to speak Norwegian.

PRESS I said, What about the Sixth Commandment?

OLA The Sixth Commandment! Phooey! That commandment is nothing to worry about.

PRESS Ha, ha, ha, ha. Well, my dear friend, is there a commandment in the Synod that says "thou shalt not drink"?

OLA Oh far from it, I've told you that it all depends on one's belief.

PRESS Well then, perhaps you'll take a drink with me?

OLA Drink? You mean a "drink" with you?

PRESS Yes, a drink.

OLA Are you treating?*

PRESS Yes, yes, I'll buy—isn't that a saloon over there? *(points)*

OLA Yes, that's Mr. Schweinigel's saloon. He's a German and doesn't belong to the Synod, but if he wants to risk burning in hell, that's his problem and none of my business. He serves good beer and that is the main thing, but he also has a beautiful daughter.

PRESS A beautiful daughter! Come on, let's go!

OLA Yes, but first you must promise me one thing.

---

*Using typical immigrant speech patterns, in the original manuscript Thrane has Ola using a Norwegianized American slang word, *"trite"* for "treat" or "buy for."

PRESS What's that?

OLA That you won't look at his daughter and that you won't speak to her either.

PRESS Why not?

OLA Well, you see, I'm courting that girl and I think I'll get her eventually.

PRESS Are you crazy? Would you marry a girl who doesn't belong to the Synod?

OLA Oh, once she becomes my wife, I'll force her into the Synod whether she wants to or not. The first thing I'll have to teach her will be to obey the Fourth Commandment. If she won't accept the Fourth Commandment that way, by hook or by crook, I'll teach her another way.

PRESS Is she a pretty girl?

OLA Absolutely, she's more beautiful than the sun, more beautiful than Bernt Askevold's "Ragnhild,"* and she sings sweeter than anything you have ever heard. In fact, she trills like a canary.

PRESS Really, well let's go in at once. *(takes hold of the door handle, but the door is locked. He knocks with his cane)*

Scene 3: OLA, PRESS, SCHWEINIGEL, KÄTCHEN

SCHWEINIGEL *(with an enormously fat stomach and large rear end, bright red nose, nightcap, and a long pipe. Speaks mostly common German and broken English. He opens the saloon door and comes out)*

OLA Here is a Yankee who wants something to drink and he wants to treat me, too.

---

*Ragnhild was a beautiful farmer's daughter in a popular story by Bernt Askevold, *Hun Ragnhild eller Billeder fra Söndfjord,* published in 1876 in *Skandinaven.* Askevold emigrated from Bergen in 1873, studied at Luther College, and eventually became a clergyman. His fiction focused on Norwegian peasant life and Ragnhild was a rural beauty who refused to marry a wealthy farmer because she was in love with a cotter's son, Ola. Ola eventually achieves success and wins Ragnhild when he impresses her father by eloquently criticizing Freethinkers and interpreting Christianity as transcending reason. Askevold's Ola is not unlike Thrane's Ola, but, as he makes clear, Ragnhild is not as beautiful as the saloon keeper's daughter.

SCHWEINIGEL Well! There is a meeting here today and I don't usually stay open, but I'll make an exception for a fine Yankee gentleman! *(aside)* This one seems like a fine fellow, and a Yankee besides, he'll make a fine husband for my Kätchen.

PRESS Three beers, if you please; but can't we have them out here—where it's nice and cool?

SCHWEINIGEL Yes, yes, you can have it just as you like it. *(shouts)* Kätchen!

KATE *(comes out)* What do you want, dear father?

SCHWEINIGEL Please bring us three beers.

KATE *(exits)*

SCHWEINIGEL So, where are you from?

PRESS From St. Paul—I am a reporter for the *Pioneer Press*. I understand there is some news worth reporting from this place?

SCHWEINIGEL Yes sir! There is much here worth reporting.

KATE *(comes out with three beers)*

SCHWEINIGEL Meine daughter! *(introduces)*

KATE *(curtsies flirtatiously)*

PRESS I am very happy to make your acquaintance. *(kisses her hand)*

OLA *(tries to hinder the kissing of the hand, but is pushed away by Schweinigel)*

PRESS *(to Schweinigel)* Tell me, you know a good deal about the Norwegian Synod, I would suppose?

SCHWEINIGEL Yes sir! I know a great deal. *(slowly)* But, you see, we must speak secretly about it, for if the Norwegian pastor or his Synod people hear anything, they will drive me out of the country. Oh! you don't know what kind of people these Synod people are. They are crazy, every one of them! Well, you can see for yourself. I'll give you that room there *(points upstairs)* and you can see and hear everything.

PRESS Oh, very good.

OLA *(during this entire conversation, he has tried to talk to Kätchen, but she has avoided him to the left, with him following; to the right, with him following, etc.)*

PRESS You have a pretty daughter, Mr. Schweinigel!

SCHWEINIGEL Oh yes, she is quite a pretty thing. And she can sing too. Maybe you can report about her singing, you know, write about her in the *Pioneer Press*? That would make her famous.

PRESS Well! It's hard for me to report about her singing if I've never heard her sing.

SCHWEINIGEL You can hear. Kätchen! Sing something nice for the gentleman—then he'll report about you in the *Pioneer Press*.

KATE *(bashfully)* Oh, I'm not a very good singer, but I will try to do the best I can. *(actress can choose any song. This song goes over to a quartet and should turn into a reel; all four dance into the saloon)*

Scene 4: PRESS, SCHWEINIGEL, BERNT, MRS. BERNT, JOHNNY

(Bernt wears ministerial robes; his wife, dressed in black, pale, limps slightly. Bernt and his wife enter from the right, accompanied by their son, Johnny)

BERNT I should have expected it, that I would hear sighing and complaining, day in and day out, nothing but sighing and complaining. Unfortunate man that I am, I suppose that I will just have to learn patience.

MRS. BERNT Dear God! How can you get so angry just because I asked you for a crutch?

BERNT Were it only a crutch, it would be no matter, but every day there is something new that must be provided. If this continues, I will be a ruined man.

MRS. BERNT But, dear God! I only asked for a simple crutch. It's been a long time since I asked you for anything.

PRESS *(is seen writing, sitting by the window on the second floor above the saloon)*

BERNT A long time since you asked me for anything? Why it hasn't even been a half year since you asked for new shoes for Johnny.

MRS. BERNT Well, he needed new shoes badly. The old ones were pretty worn out and when he has to walk many miles to school in the winter, it won't do that his feet get cold and wet.

BERNT There were Johnny's shoes, but you have also pestered me about buying a clock for the parlor? Such an unnecessary thing! When we have the Lord's own sun we have all the parlor clock we need. God created the sun in order for us to know the time, so it is, in fact, a sin to have a clock.

MRS. BERNT It's easy for you to say that a parlor clock is unnecessary, but you know how much trouble I always had because we didn't have one. But there is little point in talking about this anymore, especially since a kind man has now presented us with a parlor clock and we now have one, and you won't hear a word from me about this anymore.

BERNT And how often have you not pestered me to buy furniture, and a new stove, and only God, the Devil, and his great-grandmother know what you come up with. Had I not been the man I am, but rather been weak enough to give in to your whims and succumb to your vanity, I would have been ruined long ago. But, praise God! The Lord has given me the strength to enforce the Fourth Commandment. Furniture! When one has that which is necessary, what does one need with more?

MRS. BERNT It is easy for you to talk, for you don't know what it is to have no more than a single table, to use the same table for dining, ironing, and working on, in short, for everything. But then we need not talk about that because some of the members of the congregation were kind enough to present us with some furniture, so that's the end of that story.

BERNT End of the story, you say? As the girl said, "I'm biding my time." Oh, no, the story is not over yet, and will probably never be over, because, damn it, it won't be long before you come up with something new. As inventive as you are, I have to admit it, you will never be satisfied. It was an unfortunate day when we met each other.

MRS. BERNT That is the truest thing you have said in a long time.

BERNT Shut up!

MRS. BERNT I was just going to say—

BERNT You are just going to be quiet; when I say so, you are to be quiet! Or are you thinking of defying the Fourth Commandment?

MRS. BERNT I have never thought of defying any commandment, but the Synod's interpretation of the commandments is something else altogether.

BERNT Interpretation? So now you are planning to become an interpreter of the scriptures, too?

MRS. BERNT An interpretation must not contradict the plain meaning of the commandment.

BERNT And a wife must not contradict her husband's plain meaning—now will you hold your tongue?

MRS. BERNT But, why?

BERNT *(stamps his foot, angrily)* What the devil! Are you trying to drive me mad? If you dare to utter one more word, you better be prepared to accept the consequences.

JOHNNY *(startled by his father stamping his foot, he jumps)*

MRS. BERNT *(begins to cry)*

JOHNNY Don't cry, Mamma!

MRS. BERNT *(pats her son)*

BERNT Be quiet, boy! I don't want to hear a smart-aleck remark from you. *(to his wife)* And you will kindly control your tears until another time. Now, I see that the congregation is beginning to assemble. Don't put on such a sad, miserable face, but try to look like the others do.

MRS. BERNT That is not so easy for me.

BERNT *(stamps his foot and pulls at his hair)* Well, that's too bad. If you don't shut up, I swear I will not allow myself misfortune on your account. *(stamps his foot, angrily)*

SCHWEINIGEL *(seen in the second-floor window holding a watering can with which he sprays water into the air. Some of the water lands on Bernt just as he stamps his foot)*

BERNT *(confused)* What? Is it raining? *(looks up)* No, it's not raining. *(holds out his hand to see if it is raining)* No, not the slightest. Curious!

SCHWEINIGEL *(sprays a little more, then quickly retreats from the window)*

BERNT *(makes terrible grimaces, waves his arms and legs)* It's raining! God forgive me my sins! *(looks up)* Well! It seems to have stopped. That was the most curious rain I have ever experienced. It's like a miracle! Ah! See, there we have it, hmm, hmm. *(clears his throat, assumes a dignified, prelate-like attitude and expression)*

Scene 5: BERNT, MRS. BERNT, THE CONGREGATION

(men, women, and children enter with hymnbooks, place themselves to the right and left; the minister in the center. Individuals are designated K, L, M)

SONG NUMBER 1, Chorus

ALL

We thank you, Lord,
that you have given us
the pure, true teachings
in spite of the Evil One.
That you have sent us a minister
who teaches us the true Word,
so we can hope
that many will be saved
and that every unbeliever
will be sent to the brimstone pool
for eternity and
there be roasted and burned.
Oh Lord! Spare not
the unbeliever's soul,
the unbeliever's soul.

BERNT *(with papal expression)* My loving sheep!

ALL Amen!

BERNT Today we have a matter of great importance to deal with, and I hope the business may be conducted in the true Christian spirit, without vehemence, without bitterness, without selfishness, and without obstinacy. You know, my loving sheep, that I am meek and humble of heart and I never allow wrath or evil passions to control me.

K Allow me to call Your Reverence's attention to—

BERNT *(commanding, stamps his foot)* Quiet! Do you dare to interrupt the Lord's servant during his speech?

K *(terrified, bows deeply and is quiet)*

BERNT My loving sheep! Before we enter the meeting hall and begin our discussion, I want to point out that everyone is free to hold and express his individual opinion about the matter before us.

L Will Your Reverence allow me—

BERNT *(stamps his feet, commanding)* Quiet! Do you also dare to interrupt the servant of the Lord?

L *(worried, bows deeply and is quiet)*

BERNT I was about to say: Each of you can, of course, have and speak your individual opinion, but I bid you remember that on the day of judgment you shall be judged for every useless word you have uttered. Therefore, you must be careful as to what you say, and above all make no unnecessary objections. In general, I must call to your attention that I will present all facts which can be worthy of being presented in this matter and, after I have spoken, there can be nothing more to be said. But, I repeat, there is complete freedom for all to express their opinions.

M If there is full freedom for everyone—

BERNT *(angry, interrupts)* Have you not understood me?

M *(worried, bows deeply and is quiet)*

SONG NUMBER 2

Verse 1

BERNT

I bless you my beloved sheep

who stand steadfast in your faith,
and know that only in the Synod is salvation found.

WOMEN

We know that only in the Synod is salvation found.

MEN

And therefore do we stand on the Synod's ground.

ALL

We know that only in the Synod is salvation found,
and therefore men and women
to the Synod we are bound.

Verse 2

BERNT

And if you most would please the Lord,
you must obey his Word
and faithfully keep his Fourth Command.

WOMEN

We all will faithfully keep God's Fourth Command.

MEN

We all will faithfully keep God's Fourth Command.

ALL

We all will faithfully keep God's Fourth Command.
We will all strive to keep
God's Fourth Command.

Verse 3

BERNT

The man is woman's head, I say,
and therefore women must obey
and never contradict their husband dear.

WOMEN

And never contradict our husband dear.

MEN

A wife can never contradict her husband dear.

ALL

A wife must never contradict her loving husband dear.

(everyone enters the meeting house: led by Bernt and Mrs. Bernt, the congregation follows)

SCHWEINIGEL *(sprays water over the congregation, everyone looks up, some begin to shout, "Rain!" as they storm into the house)*

END OF ACT ONE

Act II

Same scene setting as Act 1.

Scene 1: BOYS A, B, C, D

SONG NUMBER 3, Chorus

ALL

It is a must, we must have more to drink
to have this day be merry.
Of thirsty throats we will not think
and then we'll be most cheery.

A and B

But money we must have.

C and D

But, where will it come from?

A and B

Yes, money we must have
and quite a lot at that.

ALL *(half marching, half dancing)*

And of the Conference
should it now come here,
we will send it packing
without any trouble.
Yes, we'll teach them what Norwegian boys can do.
We'll teach them what Norwegian boys can do.

A So, let's agree then to have a lively evening.

B Absolutely, a lively evening. It's been a long time since we did some carousing.

C Let's go into Schweinigel's saloon, and maybe we can do some carousing with Kätchen, too. She is the devil of a pretty girl.

A Carousing with Kätchen! No, you won't get anywhere there. She is too proud and independent these days, and that is a downright shame.

B Proud and independent? She has damn-well nothing to be proud of.

C Don't say that! If it's true what I've heard, she has plenty of possibilities.

D What kind of possibilities?

C You know the minister visits her from time to time.

A In order to convert her?

C To convert? Yeh, my foot!

B and D Ha, ha, ha.

C *(looks around)* Kari Braaten told me the other day that Kätchen told her that the minister has promised to marry her—when his wife dies.

A Oh, that is a lie, it is just gossip that Kari Braaten is spreading around. You know that Kari Braaten is full of gossip and nonsense.

C Well, there must be something to it—where there is smoke, there is usually a fire.

A Maybe so, but there is no smoke in that fire.

B Well, I have actually heard something similar.

A Oh, it's just lies. If the minister has proposed to anyone, it has to be Miss Olsen, because you know he's been a close friend of hers for a long time.

C That might be, but anyhow, I still think there is something between the minister and Kätchen.

A Come on, let's go inside then. We can talk with her and see if we can pump any information out of her.

B All right, let's go in, but who's treating?

A I can't treat anybody; I haven't got a cent.

C Not me, either. How about you, Halvor?

D *(feels in his pockets)* No, nothing here, and out of nothing, comes nothing.

A Well, if we don't have any money we can forget all about carousing.

B We can buy drinks on credit!

C Credit, ha, ha, ha, ha. No, Mr. Schweinigel doesn't give credit for a single cent.

A What do we do then?

D Nothing else to do but to go back home.

Scene 2: BOYS A, B, C, D, GALGEBERG

(Galgeberg enters, looks carefully around)

GALGEBERG Good evening!

A Good evening!

GALGEBERG God's peace be with you.

B Thank you, the same to you.

GALGEBERG Listen, dear friends! You are good Christians? Right?

A Of course we're good Christians!

GALGEBERG With the correct Synod spirit?

B Yes, that is for sure!

GALGEBERG So, I can depend on you?

C You can depend on us, that is certain.

GALGEBERG *(looks around)* You see! My friends. You know that a man was buried the other day, and you know this man belonged to the Conference. It is terrible to think that a Conference man lies in the same ground as a Synod man! Isn't that true?

B That is terrible!

GALGEBERG That can never be pleasing to the Lord God!

A Never in this world!

B It's an abomination!

GALGEBERG Listen, my friends! *(looks around)* Couldn't you go over to the graveyard and dig him up?

A Dig him up? What would we do with the body, then?

GALGEBERG You could just throw it over the fence into the ditch, by the road.*

(the boys look at each other)

GALGEBERG Well? What do you say?

B That's dangerous!

C I don't dare touch dead people.

A Yes, it's dangerous, but it's a scandal and a shame that a Conference man lies buried in the same ground as proper Christian folk.

GALGEBERG Yes, it is both a scandal and a shame. We cannot defend it, either for God or man. Now, my friends, are you willing?

(the boys look at each other and scratch their heads)

GALGEBERG I can understand, you have no courage. *(takes out money)* Well, here are a couple of dollars for drinks; then you will get courage enough.

A *(grabs the money, eagerly)* We'll do it tonight! You can count on us. Right boys? We'll do it!

B, C, D Yes, for sure!

GALGEBERG Good, don't be afraid, there's no risk. *(leaves)*

B When the need is greatest, help is nearest. Now, we got something to drink for anyway.

C "That was unexpected," said the cook after getting a kiss from the preacher.

---

*Code switching among Norwegian immigrants resulted in Norwegian grammar rules applied to American words. These words were subsequently conjugated as Norwegian words and became a part of the Norwegian-American vocabulary. Thrane has Galgeberg say: "Liget kunde Dere kaste over Fencet ner i Ditchen, som er ved Roaden."

A Well, now we have money, let's have a real fun evening.

B A real fun evening, and then tonight we will show that we are faithful laborers in the Synod's vineyard. *(they enter the saloon humming)*

Scene 3: Marie, Peter

(Marie enters, sings)

Song Number 4

Marie

Woeful girl that I am,
what shall I do?
Always my thoughts
are only of him.
Woeful girl that I am,
thoughts of him whom I love.
Yes, of him whom I love
and have loved since my childhood.

Peter

Let not the preachers
with cunning and kindness
still have the power
to keep us apart.

Marie

No, we must be parted.
We can never unite,
never in marriage unite.

Both

To the God of Love
we do implore:
Is there no way for us?
No way for us?

Peter Now, listen here, Marie, be reasonable.

Marie No, no, Peter, there is nothing to talk about anymore. Nothing will ever come of it. Your parents belong to the Conference and mine to the Synod. Never in eternity will my parents allow me to marry a member of the Conference. You don't know what they say about the Conference and its teaching. They say that it is the doctrine of the Devil and that all members of the Conference are going to— Ugh! I dare not say it.

PETER Oh, the Synod people have to watch out for themselves. They can thank God if they ever get as good a place in heaven as the Conference people. As far as that goes, it seems that both of them have rather dark prospects lately.

MARIE And how they talk about the Conference minister. They say that not only are his teachings false, but also— *(she looks around)*

PETER What else?

MARIE *(whispers in Peter's ear)*

PETER I can't hear you.

MARIE *(looks around)* They say that he is altogether too fond of young girls.

PETER But, I say, that is a hellish—

MARIE *(covers Peter's mouth)* Are you crazy?

PETER It's a lie. I would take an oath that our minister is as innocent as B—

MARIE *(quickly covers his mouth)* Will you keep still?

PETER Well, just as innocent as I am.

MARIE As you are? Ha, ha, ha, ha. No, I have to laugh. Ha, ha, ha, ha.

PETER But, when it comes to that, I can tell you something about your minister that would fill both *Budstikken* and *Skandinaven** with... "excitement and merriment" for many months.

MARIE You think so?**

PETER I think so.

---

*Norwegian-American newspapers, *Budstikken* in Minneapolis and *Skandinaven* in Chicago. These papers covered the Muus affair extensively. Thrane followed developments through the pages of *Skandinaven*. For an analysis of the newspaper coverage, see Kathryn Ericson, "Triple Jeopardy: The Muus vs. Muus Case in Three Forums," *Minnesota History* 50 (Winter, 1987) 298–308.

**Here Marie and Peter shift briefly from Norwegian to English in the original.

MARIE I think you are mistaken, Peter.

PETER I think not, Marie.

MARIE What do you know then?

PETER You want to know it?

MARIE Of course.

PETER *(looks around, whispers in her ear)*

MARIE *(boxes his ears)*

PETER Ouch! Ouch! Ouch!

MARIE You're lying.

PETER I don't lie.

MARIE You are lying!

PETER I am not.

MARIE You should be ashamed of yourself for saying such things about a man like Pastor Bernt. Why he's the senior minister in the whole Synod. There is no one like him in all of Vesterheim.* He teaches the one pure Lutheran faith and gives us the pure unadulterated milk.

PETER Milk?

MARIE Yes, the milk of the Word.

PETER Oh, the "milk of the Word," but doesn't he also give you the blood now and then, too?

MARIE Oh, yes, we get blood too, that is to say, red wine, because, naturally, nobody can drink blood.

PETER Red wine is much better. But, we weren't talking about blood or red wine, but about your minister. I can swear that he... *(whispers in her ear)*

MARIE *(slaps her hands together)* Peter, are you crazy?

PETER *(gives a throat-cutting gesture)* As sure as I stand here, a sinner in the eyes of God.

---

*"Vesterheim," literally, "the western home." This was the name used to refer to Norwegian America, the western home of the Norwegians.

MARIE Oh dear God, if this is true, then it is surely too bad.

PETER It is true! Surely you've heard a little about how he treats his wife?

MARIE Yes, I have heard a little of this and that—that he is supposed to be a terrible tyrant to his wife.

PETER Listen, Marie, let's forget about both the Synod and the Conference and get married.

MARIE Forget about the Synod and the Conference? Are you crazy? I suppose we should go over to the Swedish religion?

PETER No, no, I mean we should separate ourselves from all possible clergy.

MARIE Separate from all possible clergy? Have you totally lost your mind?

PETER We can live without the ministers. If we are honorable people and do right by everyone, we can live and die in peace.*

MARIE Peter! Peter! I understand that you are on the road to destruction—God have mercy on your soul.

PETER Well, Marie, I can see that there is no possibility with you, and that we can't think about each other any more. The best we can do is to not see each other again.

MARIE Never see each other again? That will be difficult, Peter, but when we cannot marry, then it is sensible to not see each other again.

PETER Goodbye then, Marie!

MARIE Goodbye then, Peter!

(Press is seen constantly writing)

SONG NUMBER 5

PETER

Farewell, farewell,
to you my love, so dear,
where parting is so hard to bear.

---

*Here, Peter articulates Thrane's own "Freethinker" point of view.

MARIE

We cannot wed,
our lives must be apart.
Yes, we must part.

BOTH

Hope, my dear friend,
is all we have until the end,
and all we'll ever have.

PETER Farewell, Marie! *(starts to go)*

MARIE Peter!

PETER *(returns)* Do you want something?

MARIE You're welcome to a parting kiss.

PETER Thank you, Marie! *(hugs and kisses her)*

MARIE No, now I regret that I gave you a kiss.

PETER You regret it? Well, then you better take the kiss back.

MARIE Yes, it is best that you give it back to me. *(they hug and kiss each other)*

(the boys in the saloon break out in guffaws, Peter and Marie run out)

Scene 4: BOYS A, B, C, D, PETER and a pair of Conference boys, SCHWEINIGEL

BOYS A, B, C, D *(come out of the saloon, drunk)* La la terall erall erall la, la—

SONG NUMBER 6

Verse 1

BOYS

We are drunk and full of manly courage,
and we are looking for some fun.
We want to fight, and we're not afraid of shedding blood
no matter where it comes from.
Here are Norwegian boys, we're telling you,
who can give a whipping, you should fear.

Here is Norseman strength, *hutetu*!*
Woe to any who dare come near!

Verse 2

If we should meet Conference people,
we will show them
that we can teach them a lesson from the Synod folk
as they have never before been taught.
Here are Norwegian boys, we're telling you,
we can give a whipping, you should fear.
Here is Norseman strength, *hutetu*!
Woe to any who dare come near!

A Hey, boys! Tonight I have courage! Even if ten Yankees should come, I would show them what a Norwegian can do. *(punches the air, hits the bench, and falls)*

B Tonight, I want to fight!

C Yes, me too! Tonight I won't stop until I see blood!

D Say, boys! Do you see who's coming there?

A Looks like three loafers.

C Why if it isn't three boys who belong to the Conference. Let's have some fun with them.

B Come on, let's have a little catechization.**

(Peter and a couple of other boys come in)

A Good— hic— good evening, most honorable, most worthy Conferents.

B So, the Conference is out walking today?

PETER The Conference has the same rights as the Synod.

A Same as the Synod, you say? What do you mean by that?

PETER Don't you understand Norwegian?

---

*The word *Hutetu* cannot be adequately translated in this context. It is a Norwegian word used to express a sense of exuberance or surprise that can also be a mild expletive.

**It was the custom among Norwegian-American Lutherans for children, and occasionally adults, to recite the catechism in public gatherings of the congregation in question-and-answer form.

A Don't I understand Norwegian? I understand Norwegian a lot better than any lout from the Conference.

PETER Lout, you say? Are you trying to goad me into a fight?

B Are you trying to goad us into a fight?

PETER The Synod has gotten a lot to drink today, I understand.

A Plenty to drink? What business is that of yours? We pay for our own drinks.

B *(to Peter)* You better watch out what you say about the Synod.

PETER Is that so?

A Yes, something might happen. *(makes a fighting motion)*

PETER What could happen?

A I could take a notion to cream you!

PETER Perhaps you're made of the same stuff as your minister, that you want to cream people with patience?

A What did you say? *(makes movements to fight, and Peter responds with similar movements. B and Peter make motions to each other, but nothing comes of it. Finally, all are making motions to fight. Finally, fighting breaks out with all involved)*

Music forte

(everyone is wrestling on the ground, trying to hit each other, pulling hair and tugging, all being as comical as possible)

Music piano

SCHWEINIGEL What's going on here? A battle between the Synod and the Conference? I'll cool off the loafers. *(goes in, fetches the water sprayer, sprays the boys with two strong squirts)*

Music forte

(the boys make terrible faces and run out on all fours, the Synod to the right and the Conference to the left)

Scene 5: SCHWEINIGEL, KÄTCHEN

SCHWEINIGEL *(sits on a chair outside the saloon)* Kätchen! Kätchen!

KATE *(comes out)* What do you want, dear Father?

SCHWEINIGEL I am so thirsty. I have just now cooled off a dozen loafers.

KATE Cooled off a dozen loafers, you say?

SCHWEINIGEL I mean these boys of the Synod and the Conference, you know these Norwegians here in Goodhue County, they're all crazy! Now, Kätchen, tell me, how are things going with you and that Yankee? Is he very much in love?

KATE In love? Is he very much in love with me, you mean?

SCHWEINIGEL Of course I mean in love with you. In love! Don't you understand German anymore, my child?

KATE Dear father! Please don't speak "Dutch" anymore; I hate the "Dutch" language, and I hate being called "Dutch."

SCHWEINIGEL Kätchen! Kätchen! Are you ashamed of your mother tongue? The German language is the most beautiful language in the world!

KATE No, no, the "Dutch" language is the poorest language in the world, and it is so common to talk "Dutch." I want to be an American lady, and therefore I will talk English.

SCHWEINIGEL Oh, Kätchen, Kätchen. You cause me so much worry. But, tell me now, is this Yankee very much in love? In love with you, I mean.

KATE To be sure, he is in love with me. But that is of no use, I don't want him.

SCHWEINIGEL Of no use? What are you saying? Isn't this Yankee good enough? Kätchen, Kätchen, you will end up waiting so long that you will become an old maid.

KATE No need to worry about that, dear Father. I'm already engaged!

SCHWEINIGEL What!? What did you say? Engaged?

KATE Well, not completely engaged, just sort of half engaged.

SCHWEINIGEL And all this without my permission, Kätchen! Kätchen!

KATE My sweetheart is a Norwegian.

SCHWEINIGEL What!? A Norwegian! Oh, that is too bad. But surely not a Synod man?

KATE Yes, yes, a Synod man.

SCHWEINIGEL How old is he?

KATE Oh, I don't know— about fifty years old, I guess.

SCHWEINIGEL Fifty years old! Have you lost your senses, child?

KATE He's a very good man.

SCHWEINIGEL When do you plan to be married?

KATE Married? Oh! That might be some time, because, you see, he can't marry before his wife is dead.

SCHWEINIGEL What? He is a married man? Oh Kätchen! Kätchen! You will send me to my grave. Water! Water! *(falls back on the chair)*

KATE *(brings water)*

SCHWEINIGEL What is this fellow's name?

KATE Pastor Bernt!

SCHWEINIGEL Pastor Bernt! I am dying! *(Schweinigel collapses, the music rises. Kätchen runs after beer, and pours it on him. The music stops)*

SCHWEINIGEL *(recovers)* Kätchen! Kätchen! What have you done?

KATE Dear father, be sensible. Take into consideration that Pastor Bernt is a rich man.

SCHWEINIGEL *(gets halfway up)* A rich man, you say?

KATE To be sure, he is rich.

SCHWEINIGEL Well, how rich is he, then?

KATE Well! I can't exactly tell, but I am sure he is worth $25,000.

SCHWEINIGEL $25,000? *(rises all the way up)* Kätchen, you are not as dumb as I thought at first.

(it begins to get dark)

KATE I expect him here tonight, after it is dark. We have made an appointment, he has to be nearby; then, when I commence to sing, that's my sign to him that there are no strangers here, and that I am ready to receive him.

SCHWEINIGEL $25,000 you said?

KATE Yes, $25,000—at least!

SCHWEINIGEL Then you better commence to sing as soon as possible. Hurry up!

KATE Go on, Father. He won't appear as long as you are standing here. Go in!

(Schweinigel goes into the saloon. Kate begins to sing a song)

Scene 6: KÄTCHEN, BERNT, PRESS, SCHWEINIGEL, MRS. OLSEN

(Bernt in his clerical robes is seen in the background, stealing forward. When Kätchen finishes her song, he comes forward)

BERNT Kätchen!

KATE Darling!

SONG NUMBER 7

BERNT

Are you alone?

KATE

Yes, quite alone.
How I long to see my suitor.
Oh, come nearer, you my dear.

BERNT

I fear—

KATE

There is nothing here to fear, my friend,
come you near!
There is no living being here to see us.
No, no, we are quite alone.

BERNT

Then I am here!

KATE

How I love to see my suitor,
and in love, my only tutor,
only tutor.

BERNT

Oh, my darling!

KATE

You love me?

BERNT

Passionately!

KATE

And you never will deceive me?

BOTH

In your house as wife,
your beloved wife I will be,
I will be, I will be.
You will love me night and morning,
I your house will be adorning.
You will love me night and morning,
You will love me, my dear, day and night!
Oh, what pleasure! What
charming delight!
Oh, my darling,
how I love you.
You will love me, my dear,
day and night!
Oh, what delight!
Oh, what delight!
You will love me, by day and by night.

(Press leans halfway out of the window in order to see. Schweinigel comes out)

SCHWEINIGEL *(bows very low)* Honorable pastor of the honorable Norwegian Synod. Welcome to my house!

BERNT I am glad to see that you know how to receive and honor a servant of the Lord. That shows that there is within you something of the

Spirit of the Lord. I am sorry you do not belong to the Norwegian Synod, but I hope to see the day that you will join. For as sure as I'm standing here, there is no salvation outside of the Synod.

SCHWEINIGEL Honorable pastor! I thank you for your kind wishes, but in regard to salvation, I don't care very much about that. All I really need in this world is a good glass of Milwaukee lager beer.

KATE *(slowly to her father)* Father! Father! How can you talk that way? *(shakes and shoves him)*

SCHWEINIGEL *(frightened)* Well, I don't mean to offend, honorable Mr. Pastor! I meant to say— that is, I mean my opinion is— I meant to say— well, by golly, I don't know myself what I meant. But, may I have the great pleasure of offering you a fresh glass of Milwaukee lager beer?

BERNT Well! I have no objection.

SCHWEINIGEL *(bows deeply and goes out)*

BERNT *(throws himself down on his knees before Kätchen)* Oh, my dear Kate! My dove, my darling, how I have longed to see you today— to see your sparkling eyes, your rosy cheeks, your pearly teeth— your auburn hair— your— your whole— you!

KATE Stand up, my darling!

BERNT Did you say, "darling"?

KATE Yes, ain't you my darling?

BERNT Oh, how sweet to hear that word from your rosy lips! Darling! Darling! You are my hope in life!—my hope in death, my consolation—my dear darling Buttercup! *(gets up as Schweinigel comes out with beer and they all drink, clinking glasses)*

SONG NUMBER 8

Verse 1

BERNT

Precious, dear Katrine,
I assure you, come hell or high water,
that you are my dear companion.
Oh! you are my dearest treasure,

there is no one like you to be found,
I dream about you every night.

KATE

In return I'll always love you.

SCHWEINIGEL

My daughter is so beautiful!

BERNT and KATE

None, my dear, there is above you.

ALL

With you life is only fun.
With you life is only fun.

(all three dance in a chain)

SCHWEINIGEL

My daughter is so beautiful!

BERNT

I am full of inflammation!

KATE

Will it be of long duration?

BERNT

None my dear, there is above you.

KATE

In return, I will always love you.

ALL

Now away with lamentation,
while the heart is full of mirth.
For an innocent flirtation
nobody indeed can hurt.

Verse 2

KATE

Darling, you don't know my feeling,
you my heart and soul are stealing.
Never mind the people's slander,
you will always be my friend.

You will be my dear commander
and my husband to the end.

BERNT

Boundless is my admiration.

SCHWEINIGEL

My daughter is so beautiful!

(all three dance in a chain)

Verse 3

SCHWEINIGEL

I can see, my pious children,
you love truly. Fear not
that I shall try to interfere
with your love, your heart's desire.
You have Cupid as your guide.
Breast can rest on loving breast.

BERNT

Oh, I'm feeling like a tomcat!

SCHWEINIGEL

My daughter is so beautiful!

KATE

Oh, you are such a kind, good father!

BERNT

You are such a kind, good father!

BERNT and KATE

Life with you is only fun!

SCHWEINIGEL

My daughter is so beautiful!

(all three dance in a chain)

MRS. OLSEN *(has entered toward the end and sees the dance, shows her anger, comes forward)* Well, well! So I meet the pastor in such good spirits tonight?

BERNT *(confused)* Hm! Hm! Mrs. Olsen! I had not expected to see you here.

MRS. OLSEN The pastor has obviously not expected me.

BERNT Hm! Hm! Wha— wha— wha— what the hell do you want?

MRS. OLSEN I just wanted to watch the pastor's dancing practice.

BERNT Beware, Mrs. Olsen, that the Lord Sabaoth is not offended.

MRS. OLSEN I think the Lord Sabaoth is more likely to be offended by seeing the pastor dancing here in the open.

BERNT Haven't you read that David danced before the ark out in the open?*

MRS. OLSEN Oh, so it is for the Lord's sake that the pastor is dancing. I was of the impression that you were dancing for the sake of that tart over there.

BERNT What? Tart? What have I to do with her?

MRS. OLSEN Oh, Mr. Pastor— You don't have to pretend for my sake. I know you! You haven't forgotten that Saturday evening when you thought you would soon be widowed, and you wanted to marry me. Yes, that is what you said! And that is God's truth, as surely as I am standing here a sinner before God.

BERNT Silence! You brazen woman. And don't accuse a servant of the Lord!

MRS. OLSEN Brazen woman, you say! Yes, yes, that may be so. But, who, may I ask, has made me brazen? Yes, that is the pastor's doing!

BERNT Woman! Woman! If you don't cease this evil talk, I will bring you up for church discipline; and if that doesn't help I will place you under the ban of the church!

MRS. OLSEN Oh, I am afraid of neither church discipline nor ban. The pastor himself has taught me that such things aren't so dangerous anymore. I want to say, my dear pastor, that I will not tolerate that you run around with other women, and least of all with such a good-for-nothing as Katrine Schweinigel.

KATE Good-for-nothing, you say?

---

*See 2 Samuel 6:14.

MRS. OLSEN Yes, precisely, good-for-nothing. Or are you more than a good-for-nothing when you play sweetheart to the minister and prophet?

KATE I? Play sweetheart with that minister— are you looking to get beat up? *(threatens)*

MRS. OLSEN Do you want to get beat up? *(threatens back)*

KATE Come on, if you dare!

MRS. OLSEN All right! Come on!

KATE I'm ready!

MRS. OLSEN Me too!

(during the argument, Schweinigel and Bernt have walked worriedly back and forth, pulling at their hair, etc)

KATE You miserable Norwegian creature. Do you think you are anything? I will show you what you are, and I will show you what I am.

MRS. OLSEN You German tart! If you think you can take my place with the minister, you are mistaken. I will teach you!

(Kate and Mrs. Olsen attack each other. Bernt and Schweinigel try to pull them apart. Bernt pulls on Mrs. Olsen, Schweinigel pulls at Kate. With comedic manners and exaggerations, they finally manage to pull them apart. But Mrs. Olsen and Kate try to break free and attack each other again. Bernt and Schweinigel hold on to them)

SCHWEINIGEL *(finally, throws himself down on the chair)* Beer! Beer!

BERNT *(places himself between the two women to hold them apart)* Dear Mrs. Olsen, be reasonable!

MRS. OLSEN No, I don't want to be reasonable!

BERNT If you will only be quiet and good, Mrs. Olsen, then we will be good friends again, just as in the old days, and I will come to visit you again.

MRS. OLSEN Do you promise?

BERNT I promise by all that is sacred and holy.

MRS. OLSEN And you will come and see me, soon?

BERNT I shall come this week.

MRS. OLSEN Sure?

BERNT Absolutely!

MRS. OLSEN All right, then we are good friends again. *(gives him her hand)*

Music

SONG NUMBER 8½ (Same melody as song number 8.
Kate repeats her verse 2 and Mrs. Olsen sings verse 4)

Verse 2

KATE

Darling, you don't know my feeling,
you my heart and soul are stealing,
never mind the people's slander.
You will always be my friend,
you will be my dear commander
and my husband to the end.

Verse 4

MRS. OLSEN

So, now we once again are friends
and once again I know my pastor
will not forget me at all,
but on Saturday night, on me he'll call.
How his glance, his pious voice
can melt a woman's soul!

BERNT

Again, I will be courting you.

MRS. OLSEN

Once again, he will court me.

KATE

But don't forget the lovely Kätchen!

SCHWEINIGEL

Don't forget the lovely Kätchen!

BERNT

Again, I will court you!

MRS. OLSEN

Again, he will court me!

KATE

Again, he will court me!

BERNT, KATE, and MRS. OLSEN

Life with you is only fun!

SCHWEINIGEL

My daughter is so beautiful!

CURTAIN FALLS
END OF ACT II

Act III

Livingroom in the parsonage.

Scene 1: MRS. BERNT

(Mrs. Bernt is dressed in black, is pale. Sits and knits socks)

SONG NUMBER 9

Verse 1

MRS. BERNT

We find it always too easy to believe
that where power and riches are,
there is also happiness.
But, where burdens are always light,
how blind can we be;
we never seem to learn
that all that glitters bright
is not gold, is not gold.
Where the Word of Christ is learned,
there love we also nourish.
There live piety and virtue
especially in the parsonage.
(interlude)
There Goodness should be the rule
and hear the angels' choir.

Verse 2

In pain and anguish I have strived.
For twenty years I've suffered here,
enduring all that life has given
and surely soon the end draws near.
How blind can we be;
We never seem to learn
that all that glitters bright
is not gold, is not gold.
Oh, that the Word of Christ always
would shine for me by night and day,
sure in my faith and my desires,
sure in my faith in Scripture's Word.
(interlude)
With the world's all-loving Father
to hear in bliss the angels' choir.

Scene 2: MRS. BERNT, JOHNNY

MRS. BERNT There, I am finished with these stockings. Now I have four pair of stockings ready to sell. I always get 75 cents a pair, that will be $3.00. What shall I do with the $3.00? Let me see. I very badly need a dress. I could get a simple calico dress for $2.00, and I would still have $1.00 left. But, no, first and foremost I have to get shoes and boots for little Johan, poor boy! He has to walk in snow and cold without proper footwear. It's no wonder he has been so sick lately. Yes, yes, first footwear for my little Johnny, then there will be plenty of time to think about a calico dress for myself.

JOHNNY *(enters)* Mama! My feet are so wet!

MRS. BERNT Are your feet wet, my boy? Well, it's no wonder, your boots are so bad. Otherwise, how are you today, my boy?

JOHNNY I don't think I'm well, Mama! I feel unwell, and my head is so warm.

MRS. BERNT *(feels his forehead)* Oh, my God! You have a fever, my boy. You must stay home from school and go to bed.

JOHNNY I don't dare stay home from school without asking Papa.

MRS. BERNT Well then, ask Papa.

JOHNNY Is Papa in his office?

MRS. BERNT Yes, he is, go up to him.

(Johnny leaves)

Scene 3: MRS. BERNT, KARN, HANSEN

KARN *(enters. Because she is deaf and does not speak, she uses sign language to say that someone is coming)*

MRS. BERNT *(answers with sign language that they can come in)*

HANSEN *(enters)* Good day, Madam. How are you today?

MRS. BERNT Oh, as you see, thank you.

HANSEN Is your leg no better?

MRS. BERNT No, if anything, it's worse.

HANSEN You poor thing! You certainly don't have it easy!

MRS. BERNT *(sighs)* God knows that things are not too well with me, but I guess I have to accept my lot.

HANSEN Let me tell you right out, I couldn't accept it, and even if I could, I wouldn't. Even the Fourth Commandment must have a reasonable boundary.

MRS. BERNT Well, to tell you the truth, that is my opinion, too. I am beginning to get a bit weary and am seriously thinking of ending it.

HANSEN That you should do, Madam. It has to end! The time for a break must come sooner or later and it might just as well be sooner. About the $4000: I have spoken with a fine lawyer and he says that when you want the money, your husband cannot deny your right to have it.

MRS. BERNT That is my opinion, too! It is better to divorce than to live such a life year in and year out. I would have left long ago, if it hadn't been for the scandal it would cause. Naturally, it will give rise to considerable indignation.

HANSEN Very true, indignation will come, but consider where it comes from.

MRS. BERNT As God is my witness, I am not the source of the trouble.

HANSEN I know that very well, dear Madam. Hm, hm, by the way, my wife was in town the other day, and she happened to buy some calico for a dress, and she asked me to take it along and ask the minister's wife not to refuse it. *(gives her a package)*

MRS. BERNT Thank you, thank you, but it is really a shame.

HANSEN If there is any shame, it is that the gift is so simple.

MRS. BERNT Well, greet your wife for me, and tell her many thanks.

HANSEN And, I have heard that the Madam needs a crutch.

MRS. BERNT Yes, I need a *real* crutch. I asked my husband for a crutch, so he got me that aspen stick over there. *(she points to an aspen stick lying on the floor)*

HANSEN *(picks up the stick and looks at it, shakes his head)* Well, Madam! If you will permit me, I will make a regular crutch for you. I will send it over tomorrow.

MRS. BERNT I am very grateful, Mr. Hansen.

HANSEN Shh! I think I hear the minister coming down the stairs. Well, I have to go. I don't know exactly why it is, but everyone fears him so that if one ordinarily had the heart of a lion, it would turn into that of a scared rabbit.

Scene 4: BERNT, HANSEN, MRS. BERNT

BERNT *(enters)* Good day, Mr. Hansen, God's peace be with you!

HANSEN *(bows deeply)* God's peace, Pastor.

BERNT Are you sick?

HANSEN Sick? Far from it? What makes the pastor ask?

BERNT You were not at the meeting the other day.

HANSEN Well, Pastor, something got in the way.

BERNT There are no excuses for neglecting the work in the Lord's vineyard.

HANSEN There are circumstances, Pastor.

BERNT *(interrupts)* There are *no* circumstances, my dear friend. The Lord demands all of our hearts and is not satisfied with only half. The Lord demands absolute submission and unqualified obedience. In order for us to know and understand this, he has given us his Fourth Commandment. The Fourth Commandment is the most important of all the commandments because only unqualified obedience shows a humble disposition that is pleasing to the Lord.

HANSEN True, Pastor, the Fourth Commandment is an important commandment.

BERNT No, not an important commandment, but *the* most important commandment, I say.

HANSEN Perhaps, but there are circumstances—

BERNT Haven't I just said that there are no circumstances?

HANSEN But, during certain extenuating circumstances—

BERNT *(stamps)* Have you come here to interpret scripture to the servant of the Lord?

HANSEN Oh, my goodness, no, Pastor!

BERNT Well, what do you want then?

HANSEN Ah, I— that is, I came to— that is— my wife asked me to stop by the minister's wife and present her with some cloth for a dress.

BERNT *(feels the cloth)* Dress cloth! Hm! Hm! Such material is a vanity before the Lord. What an ostentatious pattern! Look at this: flowers and leaves and other curlicues and flourishes. Listen here, Mr. Hansen! Tell your wife for me that it is very kind of her to give my wife cloth for a dress, especially now when my wife is in need of a dress, but, tell her before she bought this material, she should have read what Solomon says in Ecclesiastes about vanity.* If she had read it, she would have bought a plainer cloth. Am I not right?

HANSEN Well, Your Reverence, I—

BERNT *(stern)* Am I not right?

HANSEN Well, it depends on—

---

*See Ecclesiastes 1:2.

BERNT *(stamps and screams)* Am I not right?

HANSEN *(jumps high in fright, bows humbly)* Yes, yes, Pastor, you are perfectly right.

BERNT That is my opinion. I never say anything that is not right. Everything my mouth utters is right. I do not say this out of pride or vanity; for myself, I have no cause for self-praise, as I have nothing that I have not received. All that I say and speak, I receive from the Lord, and therefore it cannot be other than right. Am I not right?

HANSEN Well, but—

BERNT Am I not right?

HANSEN It could be—

BERNT *(angry)* Am I not right, I say?

HANSEN *(afraid)* Yes, yes, your Reverence. Well, I must go. Farewell! *(begins to go)*

BERNT Wait! Tell me, Mr. Hansen! I hope you have a couple of extra dollars for Decorah College?*

HANSEN Oh, certainly, Reverend Pastor. *(takes out money)* Here is $10.00. *(wants to go)*

BERNT Wait! It is a long time since you contributed to the mission.

HANSEN *(takes out money)* I don't think it's so long ago, but if the pastor wishes—

BERNT Excuse me! It is not *I,* but the *Lord* who wishes it.

HANSEN Well, here is $5.00.

BERNT A man in your position should be able to give $10.00.

HANSEN Oh, God of Abraham! *(gives more)* Well! Now I must go. Farewell! Farewell!

BERNT Wait! It is necessary to paint the parsonage. It hasn't been painted for eight years. Since there is no money in the treasury, the money must come in by collection. I hope you will contribute.

---

*Bernt is referring to Luther College, Decorah, Iowa, the leading Norwegian-American educational institution in the 1880s.

HANSEN Oh, for goodness sakes! Has the pastoral sack no bottom?

BERNT Now, Mr. Hansen?

HANSEN Well, Pastor, to tell you the truth, I can't afford it. The times have been tough.

BERNT You must remember that what you give will be returned to you 100-fold in heaven.

HANSEN *(aside)* If only that were certain. *(aloud)* Well, Pastor, here is $5.00, but now I have to leave. Farewell! Farewell! *(leaves)*

BERNT Ha, ha, ha, ha! Everything perishes, but stupidity endures! It is truly remarkable that people can be so dumb. Still, I'll be damned if this Mr. Hansen is so dumb, but he is a moral coward, just like all the others. Ha, ha, ha, ha! People's stupidity and cowardice enable us ministers to live in ease and comfort. We rule the stupid by lies and the cowardly by audacity. By lies and audacity is the world ruled.

Scene 5: BERNT, MRS. BERNT, HANSEN

(Hansen enters sneaking through the door after Bernt has begun his song)

SONG NUMBER 10

Verse 1

BERNT

Wherever you go in any land
there's nothing to compare with the Synod grand,
all quake with fear of the Synod's ban!
And willingly obey their clergyman!

MRS. BERNT and HANSEN

For everything there is a time,
That must be understood.

BERNT

Yes, worldly things will pass away,
but man's stupidity will always stay.

MRS. BERNT and HANSEN

For everything there is a time,
that must be understood.

Even human stupidity
will, one day, be gone for good.

Verse 2

BERNT

From the scripture we get all the sense,
explain it all just as it suits our plans.
And the Fourth Commandment we clearly see
as unquestionable obedience and slavery.

MRS. BERNT and HANSEN

But people wake up,
and soon say, "Enough!"

BERNT

Yes, everything will pass away,
but man's stupidity will always stay.

MRS. BERNT and HANSEN

But soon they will say stop,
when of stupidity they've had enough.
For everything there is a time,
that must be understood.

BERNT

Yes, everything will pass away,
but man's stupidity will always stay.

MRS. BERNT and HANSEN

But people will wake up
and then they will say "Stop!"
Even human stupidity
will, one day, be gone for good.

Verse 3

BERNT

The stupid people are ready
to swallow all we say, then much more.
Yes, they'll swallow it up, however false it be,
we give them what they want; they neither hear nor see.

MRS. BERNT and HANSEN

Remember even human stupidity
will, one day, be gone for good.

BERNT

Yes, worldly things will pass away,
but man's stupidity will always stay.

MRS BERNT and HANSEN

But people will wake up,
and then they will say, "Stop!"
Even human stupidity
will, one day, be gone for good.

Verse 4

BERNT

Whatever opinions you might express,
a preacher is a preacher, you must confess.
He teaches scripture as he chooses to,
what's the wildest is the likeliest to be thought true.

MRS. BERNT and HANSEN

For everything there is a time,
that must be understood.

BERNT

Yes, everything will pass away,
but man's stupidity is here to stay.

MRS. BERNT and HANSEN

But people will wake up,
and then they will say, "Stop!"
Even human stupidity
will, one day, be gone for good.

Verse 5

BERNT

Oh, nothing can compare with the clergyman's state,
as most honored of professions, his must rate.
The clergyman, respected and feared,
at his request, all is gladly volunteered.

MRS. BERNT and HANSEN

For everything there is a time,
that must be understood.
Even human stupidity
will, one day, be gone for good.

BERNT

Yes, everything will pass away,
but man's stupidity will always stay.

MRS. BERNT and HANSEN

But the people will wake up,
and then they will say, "Stop!"
Even human stupidity
will, one day, be gone for good.

Verse 6

BERNT

A minister in his home must rule,
and to rule his wife must like a cat be cruel.
When the cat's away, then the mouse* will play,
and, therefore, he must tame the woman night and day!

MRS. BERNT and HANSEN

For everything there is a time,
that must be understood.

BERNT

A wife cannot rule the house,
she must be tamed, like cat tames mouse.

MRS. BERNT and HANSEN

The wife, she will wake up,
and then she will say, "Stop!"
Even a woman's patience
will, one day, be gone for good.

(Hansen sneaks out, quickly)

---

*Thrane uses the word "Muus," meaning mouse, but it is also the last name of Bernt Muus, the Lutheran minister of the real Holden Church, on whom the play is based.

Scene 6: MRS. BERNT, BERNT, KARN

MRS. BERNT Listen, my husband, are you going to town today?

BERNT Yes, I am. Why?

MRS. BERNT I have such pain in my leg today.

BERNT Oh, that old story! There's always something lacking, always whimpering and complaining!

MRS. BERNT I just wanted to ask you to stop by the drugstore.

BERNT The drugstore again? I should have expected it!

MRS. BERNT I wanted to ask you if you would buy some salve for my leg.

BERNT Buy and buy! Never anything but "buy"! If this doesn't stop, I'll be a ruined man!

MRS. BERNT Oh, for God's sake! A little salve to rub on my leg can't cost anymore than 10, 20 cents.

BERNT 10, 20 cents here and 10, 20 cents there; never an end to 10, 20 cents! I am *not* going to the drugstore!

MRS. BERNT But I *must* have something to salve my leg with.

BERNT You, you, you— You will have to salve yourself with patience.*

MRS. BERNT Patience? Yes, I've shown that for nearly twenty years.

BERNT Yes, patience is a real virtue, or have you not read in the scriptures that it is necessary to exercise patience in times of suffering?

MRS. BERNT I thought I had shown enough patience in these twenty years. It doesn't really matter; with my work, I'll be able to buy my own salve for my leg. But, there is something I would like to ask you about.

BERNT Now, again? Is there no end to your demands?

MRS. BERNT You travel so often to Norway to visit relatives and friends. Couldn't I also be allowed, just once, to travel to Norway to visit my relatives and friends?

BERNT *(astonished)* What...is...that? *You* travel to Norway? Are you crazy?

---

*"To salve (or butter) yourself with patience" is a Norwegian idiom for "Be patient!"

MRS. BERNT Is it less than reasonable that I, too, get to visit relatives and friends?

BERNT Listen, wife! It is apparent that you are losing your mind. Instead of sending you to Norway, I think it would soon be best to send you to St. Peter!*

MRS. BERNT But a wife must, nevertheless, also have rights. A wife—

BERNT Shut up!

MRS. BERNT A wife must—

BERNT *(stamps)* Shut up! I do not want to hear any more! *(leaves)*

MRS. BERNT *(alone)* My God! How long will my torment last? Oh, how difficult it is to maintain proper meekness under such conditions. My patience is so constantly tested that I fear it will one day break.

KARN *(enters, frightened, making signs that something has been broken into pieces)*

MRS. BERNT What is it now?

KARN *(repeats the same signs)*

MRS. BERNT I don't understand what you mean.

BERNT *(enters, angrily)* No, this is really too much! This is going too far! Again, I have found a water mug broken. You left it overnight with water in it, and the water has frozen, breaking the mug in two. Everything gets broken and destroyed in this house. You have no forethought! I shall become a ruined man. Have I not told you a hundred times that you must pay more attention to the affairs of the house? But you do not obey. You despise the Fourth Commandment. Don't you know that a wife is supposed to obey her husband and submit to her husband?

MRS. BERNT Submit and obey, even if the husband's commands are unreasonable?

BERNT A wife must not allow herself to judge whether her husband's commands are reasonable or unreasonable. A wife must obey blindly.

---

*St. Peter, Minnesota, the site of the Minnesota State Mental Hospital.

When a husband says, "Go!" then she must go. If he says, "Stop!" then she must stop. She must do whatever he says.

MRS. BERNT And when he says, "Freeze and starve," then I suppose she must freeze and starve?

BERNT Yes, she must!

MRS. BERNT My dear friend! You must pardon me, but that is not the way I understand the Fourth Commandment.

BERNT What...is...that? You dare to interpret scriptures in your own way and contradict a servant of the Lord?

MRS. BERNT I have begun to doubt whether you really are a servant of the Lord.

BERNT Wha— Wha— What...is...that? You dare? *I*, not a servant of the Lord? Whose servant do you take me for?

MRS. BERNT I am afraid that you serve the Evil One more than you serve the Lord.

BERNT *(raging)* No! Now, now, now, now you have gone too far. Do you have no conscience? No religion?

MRS. BERNT Religion? If your way of thinking and acting is religion, then I believe it would be best for mankind to have no religion.

BERNT You! You! You! I— *(charges his wife)*

Music

KARN *(jumps between them making lively gestures)*

BERNT *(makes signs telling Karn to get out of the room)*

KARN *(stamps the floor, and remains)*

BERNT *(stamps the floor, pulls Karn's hair and throws her toward the door)*

KARN *(returns to her position, placing herself in front of Mrs. Bernt with crossed arms and "fire" in her eyes. She leaves when Mrs. Bernt begins to speak)*

MRS. BERNT Was this also a display of religion?

BERNT Listen here! Now there is no alternative but to send you to St. Peter. You shall be sent to St. Peter, tomorrow!

MRS. BERNT I am not going to St. Peter, but I am going to Norway! Now, I will tell you right out that I will be patient no longer. The time for my patience is passed. Now, I want my inheritance, the $4000 you have in your possession.

BERNT *(stamps and pulls at his hair)* No! This gets worse and worse! Listen, wife! Don't you try my patience. You could make me furious. You will not get the $4000, not a cent of it!

MRS. BERNT But, I demand it! It is *my* money!

BERNT *Your* money?! No money is your money! A wife has no right to own anything for herself. Everything a woman has belongs to her husband.

MRS. BERNT Then you will not give me my 4000 dollars?

BERNT Oh! Go to St. Peter!

MRS. BERNT Good, if you won't give it to me willingly, I will have to take legal action.

BERNT Legal action? You, you, you— *(confused and desperate, unable to speak because of anger)*

MRS. BERNT Yes, I am taking legal action. Everthing must have an end, and so too my oppression must come to an end.

BERNT Listen, wife! Since Satan has gotten such power over you, I can no longer save you. I will have to bring you up before the congregation and have you placed under church discipline.

MRS. BERNT I am not afraid of the church's discipline. In any case, it will not be as oppressive as your house discipline.

BERNT You shall be cast out of the Synod.

MRS. BERNT Well, then I shall, at least, be in good company.

BERNT Good company, you say?

MRS. BERNT Yes, the way you and yours carry on, the end will probably see the best members leaving the Synod and agreeing on a purer doctrine than the Synod offers.

KARN *(enters, making signs that people are coming)*

Scene 7: BERNT, MRS. BERNT, TOSKEBERG, ASENBY, FAARELUND, RÆVELAND

(the four Synod ministers enter with members of the congregation.)

BERNT Oh, my brothers in Christ! You have come at the most opportune moment! Today, it is my sad duty to accuse my own wife before the congregation, so that she can—

TOSKEBERG What do we hear? What can this mean?

RÆVELAND Has the Evil One gained power over her heart?

BERNT Yes, Satan himself has gained power over her. She not only rejects the clear Word of scripture, but she even denies it. She denies the Fourth Commandment, and says that a wife does not need to subject herself to her husband.

TOSKEBERG What can we be hearing?

RÆVELAND This is terrible to hear. *(to Bernt)* My poor brother, who has gotten this evil into your house!

ASENBY When a wife sinks so deeply into sin, there is nothing else to do but to bring her under severe church discipline!

BERNT Imagine! The Evil One has taken control to such an extent that she has even demanded the payment of $4,000, which she received as an inheritance a few years ago.

ASENBY Is this possible? *(clasps his hands together)*

RÆVELAND *(clasps his hands together)* Is this possible?

ASENBY This just proves the fruits of the American way of thinking and of today's pernicious enlightenment.

RÆVELAND And of American liberty!

BERNT And of the American common school!

ASENBY Only now do I fully realize the truth in Pastor Preus's* statement that the natural sciences are a deadly poison.

BERNT My brothers! Hereafter, we must be stricter than ever! We must

*Hans Amberg Preus, a leader in the Norwegian Synod who had been one of the founders of the Synod in 1853.

establish as an undeviating rule never to give communion to anyone who allows their children to attend the common school, and we must never permit any farmer to board or hire anyone who does not belong to the Synod.

ASENBY Correct, Brother Bernt! Strictness is essential, the utmost strictness.

RÆVELAND Yes, the utmost stictness. No more mercy. It is unfortunate that the church no longer has the power to punish the rebellious with prison or the stake, such as in the good old days.

FAARELUND Yes, yes, it is a disappointing time in which we live. All one hears about is liberty and enlightenment. Oh you pitiful liberty and you pitiful enlightenment. But this, too, must end.

BERNT Yes, it must end, and "by Golly," it will end! The rebellious must be subjugated and humbled, and above all there will be no toleration of any violation of the Fourth Commandment. *(to his wife)* Listen, wife! Look within yourself and repent! Acknowledge your faults and promise that, in the future, you will pay heed to, and obey, the Fourth Commandment.

FAARELUND Precious sister, repent before it is too late!

ASENBY No longer try the patience of the entire congregation.

MRS. BERNT *(looks contemptuously at them)*

FAARELUND Answer, woman! Will you repent?

MRS. BERNT *(measures Faarelund with a contemptuous look)*

ASENBY Woman! Woman! Humble yourself and acknowledge your grievous sin!

MRS. BERNT *(looks at him contemptuously)*

FAARELUND Answer, woman!

ASENBY Answer, woman!

BERNT *(stamps)* Answer them, damn it!

MRS. BERNT Since you are determined to have an answer, you shall have it. My answer is this: I have had the opportunity to study the Norwegian Synod for 20 years, and I can in truth say that I know it very well, both its sheep and its shepherds. It claims that it alone has the true doctrine, but never have I seen so little of the true Christianity as I have seen among you! If Christ returned to earth, he would not recognize you as his disciples, but rather label you among the Pharisees, and call you snakes and vipers. Your Christianity is nothing more than sophistry and hairsplitting and its fruits are falsehood, hypocrisy, hardheartedness, and all manner of evil; I am no prophet, but what I have seen and experienced among you makes it easy to prophesy that through your teachings and conduct, men's hearts are not filled with faith and trust, but with mistrust and doubt. Even the most obvious Freethinkers do not contribute so much to the spread of disbelief as you ministers of the Synod.

ASENBY Brother Bernt! How long shall this woman try our patience?

RÆVELAND Woman! Woman! What are you saying? You are possessed.

MRS. BERNT I have more to say—

BERNT Be silent, I say! Not one word more!

MRS. BERNT *(commanding)* Now you shall be silent, for now it is *my* turn to speak. This is the last time I will speak to you; for now we must part. But before we part, I will let you hear that which you most hate to hear, namely the truth! And the truth is this: it will not be long before your sheep realize that you are working against liberty and enlightenment and against everything that most benefits mankind. I prophesy, therefore, that sooner than you think, your sheep will leave you, fleeing here and there. You will be left behind, forsaken as unfaithful shepherds, as unfaithful stewards of the treasures that were entrusted to you. That is my last word! Farewell! *(leaves to the left, with a dignified bearing. The congregation members also leave, so only Bernt and the four ministers remain)*

Scene 8: BERNT, the MINISTERS, KÄTCHEN, SCHWEINIGEL

(Music. The four ministers remain standing, looking at each other with comic, horrified, and sheepish faces, making comic grimaces to each other, nodding, shaking their heads)

FAARELUND Listen, Bernt! What we have to do now is adopt serious rules of procedure.

RÆVELAND One mangy sheep infects the entire herd!

BERNT Church discipline! Church discipline!

ASENBY Expulsion from the Synod!

TOSKEBERG Listen, Bernt! Your wife is a horrible sinner, that is obvious and true. However, a large part of this scandal could have been avoided if you had behaved more properly.

BERNT What are you saying? Do you dare to bring accusations against me?

ASENBY I agree with Pastor Toskeberg that this scandal could have been avoided if you behaved more reasonably.

BERNT Shut up! Or, perhaps, you too want to face church discipline?

FAARELUND Brother Bernt has behaved as a reasonable man. He has disciplined his wife, and that is proper.

TOSKEBERG I have nothing against that he kept control over his wife, a wife is a wife and needs to be controlled, but the scandal could have been avoided if Brother Bernt—

BERNT *(interrupts)* Shut up, I say! *(stamps)*

TOSKEBERG No! I will *not* shut up! I will express my opinion.

BERNT There cannot be more than one opinion on this case.

TOSKEBERG Yes, the case can be looked at from two sides. I think you should let your wife have her $4000.

BERNT *(jumps into the air)*

FAARELUND *(also jumps into the air and clasps his hands)*

BERNT May I ask: *Does* my wife have any right to the $4000?

TOSKEBERG She has no right— that is to say— before the Lord. But, what will people think?

BERNT What will people think? Ha, ha, ha, ha. As long as I have the money, I don't give a damn about what people think.

ASENBY That's easy for you to say. You not only have the $4,000, but another $20,000 as well.

TOSKEBERG Yes, it is true, Bernt has money. And because of that he can tell the world off. It's not so easy with the rest of us who have no money. We can't afford to tell the world off.

ASENBY Of course we can't. Why, what would we live off if we didn't care about what others thought?

BERNT Live off? Oh, ye of little faith! Consider the sparrows, they do not spin, they do not lay up treasures, and yet the Lord feeds them.*

TOSKEBERG No, I tell you what, Bernt. Now you have gone too far. When you compare us to sparrows, you need to watch what you say.

ASENBY We are no sparrows. We need things quite different than the sparrows. We need roasts and wine and fine horses and buggies, and pleasure trips to the Old Country now and then and, God knows all that we need.

TOSKEBERG Yes, that's true, Brother Asenby. We are not sparrows and we cannot live like sparrows. The devil! *(covers his mouth)* God forgive me my wicked sin. It would be the deuce to be a minister if one was to live like a sparrow.

BERNT Oh, ye of little faith! Ye seek that which moth and rust corrupts, ye seek the treasure of this world, instead of seeking righteousness.**

ASENBY No, you know what? Now you have become quite amusing. Are you talking about not seeking the treasures of this world, you who would willingly take a widow for her last cent?

BERNT Wha— Wha— What are you saying?

ASENBY And you aren't even satisfied with just one wife.

BERNT *(jumps high)* Are you trying to infuriate me?

ASENBY I am only saying that which is true. Or is it not true that you are in an altogether too friendly relationship with Mrs. Olsen?

BERNT *(jumps high and slaps his hands together)*

---

*See Matthew 10:29–31; Luke 12:6–7; Matthew 6:28; Luke 12:27.

**See Matthew 6:19–20.

FAARELUND *(jumps high and slaps his hands together)* Brother Asenby must be brought under church discipline!!!

ASENBY If I am to be brought under church discipline, so must Brother Faarelund.

FAARELUND Me?

ASENBY Yes, you! I can prove that you have kept false records of some of the congregational funds.

FAARELUND *(throws himself on a chair)* Water!

BERNT And you, Brother Asenby, better watch out for yourself, or do you plan to make people think that you have kept proper accounting of the mission funds that came in two years ago?

ASENBY *(throws himself on a chair)* Water!

FAARELUND Brother Asenby shall be thrown out of the Synod.

BERNT Let us throw him out at once!

TOSKEBERG No, Brother Asenby is not going to be thrown out!

FAARELUND Yes, he shall!

BERNT Come! Let us throw him out!

SONG NUMBER 11

(The chorus begins singing just as the ministers fly at one another. Bernt and Faarelund grab Asenby to throw him out, but Asenby and Toskeberg hold on to each other. General fighting breaks out as the four pull hair, hit, kick, and bite each other. The chorus sings. The public gets involved. Schweinigel enters with his sprayer and sprays the ministers)

Chorus

MEN

Our shepherds now we know,
their character is proven
as clear as day, and no
more proof we need be given.

WOMEN

So let them all to Bloksberg* go,
whatever happens to them,
we to the whole wide world must show
that we can live without them.

ALL *(repeat men's lines)*

Scene 9: HANSEN, PETER, MARIE, SCHWEINIGEL, KÄTCHEN, OLA, BERNT

HANSEN *(claps for order)*

A Quiet! Mr. Hansen has the floor!

B Mr. Hansen has the floor!

(everyone is quiet)

HANSEN Hm! Hm! My friends! You know me as the man who has long dared to think freely! I have tried from time to time to open your eyes! But of course, that was seen as lies! Instead of giving me sensible answers, you forced me out of the town. What I have not been able to do in the course of many years, our dear Pastor Bernt and his comrades have managed to do in a very short time: namely to open your eyes to the real nature of the Synod. Maybe this will open your eyes to many other things too. But since our dear Pastor Bernt has accomplished so much in such a short time, I propose three times three hurrahs, for Pastor Bernt. Hurrah!

ALL Hurrah! Hurrah! Hurrah!

HANSEN And then I suggest that you collect money for a monument for Pastor Bernt, agreed?

ALL Yes! yes!

HANSEN And the inscription on the monument ought to read thus: "Pastor Bernt. The Friend of Liberty and Enlightenment." Agreed?

ALL Yes! Yes!

---

*Refers to Brocken, the peak in the Harz Mountains of Germany where a "Witch's Sabbath" was traditionally celebrated on Walpurgis Night, April 31.

PETER *(holding Marie's hand, to Hansen)* Excuse me, aren't you the justice of the peace?

HANSEN Yes, I'm the justice of the peace.

PETER Begging your pardon. Can't you marry people as well as a minister?

HANSEN Yes, every bit as well, if not better. Perhaps you are thinking of getting married?

PETER Yes, that's it. Today the two of us got sufficient sense to see that we could marry without threatening our salvation. And since this day has become a kind of day of freedom, we thought we might as well celebrate our wedding on this day.

HANSEN That is absolutely correct. You are two reasonable human beings. *(takes a paper out of his pocket)* I happen to have a marriage form here and all you need to do is fill it out. What is your name?

PETER Peter Andersen Sønsteby.

HANSEN *(writes. Turns to Marie)* And what is your name?

MARIE Marie Hansdatter Furuland.

HANSEN *(writes)* And you have decided to enter into the fortunate state of holy matrimony with each other?

PETER and MARIE Yes!

HANSEN Very well! *(places his hands on them)* The Lord bless you; live happily and multiply.

GIRLS *(giggle, and cover their faces with their hands)*

HANSEN But, my young friend, where will the wedding be?

PETER The whole parsonage is empty now, so I'm thinking we could celebrate the wedding right here.

HANSEN Yes, why not? The parsonage belongs to the congregation and, as such, the congregation has the right to make use of it.

ALL Yes, yes.

PETER *(to Schweinigel, changing from Norwegian to English)* Mr. Schweinigel! We are going to have a wedding party here tonight. I will pay for it all.

SCHWEINIGEL All right! *(hurries out)*

HANSEN Anybody else?

KATE *(takes Ola Nauteby aside)* You, Ola! There you see a bride and bridegroom!

OLA Yes, I see that.

KATE One couple alone is not enough, there should be two, don't you think?

OLA I think so.

KATE Do you understand what I mean?

OLA I think so. Shall I ask the justice?

KATE Of course, do it!

OLA *(to Hansen)* Do you have another set of those papers on you? I mean, for marriage?

HANSEN Yes, that I have. Do you also wish to be married?

OLA Yes, that girl there and I have agreed to have a wedding this evening, too.

HANSEN That is fine. *(takes out paper)* Now, what is your name?

OLA Ola Andersen Nauteby.

HANSEN *(to Kate)* And the miss's name is?

KATE Kätchen Schweinigel.

HANSEN *(writes)* I give you my blessing. Increase and multiply.

KATE *(cuffs Hansen's ears)*

HANSEN Ouch! Ouch!

SONG NUMBER 12 (Quartet and Chorus)

(Marie and Kätchen sing together; Ola and Peter sing together)

KATE

And so I say my marriage vows
with a husband not too bright.

Though smart he may not be,
he is the man for me.

MARIE

And so I say my marriage vows;
full of reason my husband is.
In spite of churchly ban
he will be my man.

OLA

Now disappeared has clergy rule,
they can no longer fool.
Everything has turned out fine
and Kätchen will be mine.

PETER

Now disappeared has clergy rule,
folk are no more fooled.
Everything has turned out fine
and Marie will be mine.

ALL

Joyous, joyous, we must be.
They have their own true love.
Dancing we no longer fear,
each dancing with our dear.

(the two couples begin to dance, other couples follow. Bernt enters, is furious)

BERNT Stop! You children of Satan. Do you dare to profane the parsonage with dance and ungodly activity? Get out! Out!

HANSEN Honorable Pastor! We intend to have a wedding celebration here tonight and we do not intend to leave here before tomorrow morning.

BERNT Wha— Wha— What? You intend to have a wedding celebration in the parsonage? You plan to stay all night? But, I say by golly, you are to pack up this instant and leave, all of you, by golly!

HANSEN We are determined to stay here all night, and therefore, Pastor, you just have to have patience.

CHORUS

Now it's your turn to show some patience,
if you are able to.
Now it's time to show you can
be patient like a godly man.
And if you cannot stand
that we are joyous here,
then we recommend that you
go to St. Peter, Pastor dear.
Now it's your turn to show some patience,
if you are able to.
Now it's time to show you can
be patient like a godly man.

(during the song, Bernt moves threateningly at each singer, but is pushed away so that he seems like a ball thrown between them all. Eventually, he becomes so angry he grabs a chair, or something else, and wants to strike with it. At that point, Schweinigel sprays him in the face so that he falls, makes terrible facial expressions, and receives another spray. Bernt then gets to his feet and runs out as quickly as he can)

CHORUS

If it is true, that freedom is a blessing,
and enlightenment is a worthy force,
the Synod's overdue for a chastising,
and deserves correction to its course.
Vesterheim's Synod long has been opposed
to all that liberty and progress leads,
so therefore it deserves a good kick in the rear
to show them we're not sheep.
To show them that we will not bow
to any church or papal power
and we far from accept the Synod's view
of the Fourth Commandment.

Against slavery we strongly will protest
and all who fight the common school.
The time of the clergy's intolerant rule
one day soon shall end,

the clergy's dominating days
when we so patient had to be,
and God knows that we did as we were told
and practiced the virtues we were supposed to have.
We must clear away the fog of unreason
and forever let the light of reason shine.
A new day dawns and brightly shines the sun.

ALL

A new day dawns and brightly shines the sun,
light's victory is assured.
And teachings about slavery
will also have an end.
A God of joy, we worship here,
and will be forever free!
The Fourth Commandment it is clear
does not mean tyranny.
And cries for patience we will use no more
to keep another down.
Of all such plagues we weary were,
but now we will be free!

CURTAIN FALLS

THE END

The Power of the Black Book

A COMEDY

Characters:

PEER, blacksmith

ELSE, his wife

ANNE, their daughter

GUNDER, lover

ERIK, Farmer

Scene 1: PEER, ELSE, ANNE

Setting: A farmer's cottage in Norway. The door in the background is open. Outside the back door is seen a forge with a fire. Peer is blacksmithing. As the curtain rises, Anne and Else are singing a ballad which, before long, Peer begins to keep time with by his hammering on the anvil.

PEER *(following the song, he enters angrily)* See there, the small tongs are gone again. *(goes over to a box, fumbles around in it)* Damn! Who is it who's always in this box? Is it you, Anne?

ANNE Me? No. I never touch that box.

PEER *(brings up a couple of different tools, which he puts on the floor)* No, it isn't here. Why the hell can't people leave my things alone?

ANNE What is it you're looking for?

PEER My small tongs are gone. When I'm going to use something, it's always gone. Tongs don't have legs and couldn't disappear on their own. *(stamps on the floor and throws his tools)*

ELSE *(enters)* What is it? What is it?

PEER My small tongs are gone just when I need to use them. My tools always seem to disappear and then I have to buy new ones. There seems to be no end to this buying.

ELSE It's no wonder that you have to buy so many tools, you work night and day.

PEER Night and day? Night and day yourself.

ELSE Well, you do. I don't understand how you manage. Any other blacksmith would have given up long ago.

PEER Another blacksmith, maybe, but I am not just any other blacksmith!

ELSE But, why do you work so much?

PEER That's my business.

ELSE Yes, but if something happens to you, then I'll be left here alone.

PEER That's your business.

ELSE And the children will be alone.

PEER And that'll be their business.

ELSE *(takes hold of him under his chin)* For God's sake, Peer! Don't be so contrary and sour. Are you angry at someone? Are you angry at me?

PEER Angry? Angry? Why are you always asking me that? I'm not angry at anyone; I'm not angry. But I am upset.

ELSE But, what are you upset about?

PEER Well, I'm not really upset either, but I am annoyed.

ELSE But, why are you annoyed? What is it lately that you have been so unhappy? You weren't like that before.

PEER That may be. There was a time when I had some hope. But now, I'm over fifty years old and not much to show for it.

ELSE But what does money have to do with being happy?

PEER *(derisively)* Right. One has to be poor to be happy, I suppose?

ELSE Oh, who's talking about being poor. We're the last people to talk about poverty. We own this house, we have property, and you are a good blacksmith. What more could you want?

PEER What more could I want? You talk like you know something about it.

ELSE Well, I think we all do. I think it's a shame that you feel you have to complain.

PEER And if I break my arm or lose my sight or become lame or get arthritis, or something like that, so I can't work anymore—what then? Are we going to be able to live then?

ELSE Oh, you're just looking for the worst. Why should you break your arm or lose your sight any more than anyone else?

PEER Have you never heard of anyone breaking their arm or losing their sight?

ELSE Of course, I have.

PEER Well then, I could also break my arm or lose my sight.

ELSE But, dear, what would the world be like if everyone went around thinking they would become crippled?

PEER Who said that I *thought* that? I didn't say that I *thought* I would, I said that I *could*. Don't you understand that there is a big difference between the two?

ELSE Yes, but are we then to live constantly worrying about and fearing what could happen?

PEER That was well said. Perhaps we should live in fear of that which cannot happen?

ELSE For God's sake! You've been so contrary lately, Peer. You're not like you used to be.

PEER That's true. In my youth I had a smooth face, but now it's full of wrinkles. When I was young I was spry and light-footed, but now my legs are as stiff as a worn-out horse. Sometimes I can't even move because I'm so tired.

ELSE Yes, well, young people get just as tired when they work as much as you have.

PEER But, now I'm asking you again, if I become sick and can't work anymore, what then?

ELSE Well, we still have our property.

PEER Do you think we can live off that?

ELSE For God's sake, there's always a way.

PEER Well, before you know it, you'll end up on poor relief.

ELSE Should things go so badly that you can't work anymore, then we could live off our property, if Anne and I both worked too.

PEER Yes, that would be a wonderful life. As if the people over there at the Sonstevoll farm weren't already proud enough—they would have the pleasure of seeing us in poverty. And what of those over at Huseby? Do you think they would have anything to do with us if we were poor?

ELSE Ah, we can do without both the Sonstevolls and the Husebys.

PEER It's easy to talk about not having any food when the stomach is full. But, for crying out loud, listen to me, standing here wasting time. Where are those small tongs? Somebody must have taken them.

ELSE I wonder if they're not down in the stall. You were taking out some nails there the other day.

PEER Well, then go down to the stall and bring them up to me.

ELSE *(goes out)*

PEER *(throws the tools back into the box)* So, so. Well now that they're back there, maybe they'll be left alone. *(goes out)*

Scene 2: ANNE, GUNDER.

ANNE *(while spinning, she sings a verse of the same song as in the first scene)*

GUNDER *(enters)*

ANNE *(happy)* Gunder! Is it you? How unexpected!

GUNDER Unexpected! Yes, that might be. Perhaps also unwelcome?

ANNE Oh, you're always most welcome, Gunder.

GUNDER *(takes her hand)* Thank you for those words, Anne. You're the same as you've always been, I knew it. You will always be the same, as faithful as pure gold.

ANNE You seem to care as much for me, Gunder?

GUNDER You know that very well, Anne. Even though I've enjoyed the two years I've been away at school, there were many times that I missed you so much that I almost left to come home.

ANNE What is that school you've been at called?

GUNDER A Folk High School!

ANNE A Folk High School? Is that the same as an agricultural school?

GUNDER Oh no, far from it.

ANNE What do they teach at a Folk High School?

GUNDER Oh, we learn quite a lot. We get a pretty good idea about all kinds of knowledge.

ANNE Well, it's too fancy for me. Is what you learned of any use?

GUNDER All knowledge can be used for something, Anne. I thank my father because he insisted that I attend the school. I've learned so many things that I never had any idea about before. I've managed to get rid of all kinds of prejudices and foolish superstitions. I believe I feel like a slave must feel to finally be free of his chains. When I think of all the dumb stories about ghosts and gnomes and mountain trolls that I ate up so eagerly and believed as though it were gospel. When I think about how ignorant people are about nature's great works, I can only feel sorry for the simple person's intellect. It's even worse in a country like ours where the most simple farmer has so much influence on the country's well-being.

ANNE It sounds like you are now an educated man, Gunder.

GUNDER Educated? No, it takes more than that to be educated, Anne. One cannot become fully educated in just two years, but just as the catechism is an abbreviated form of the word of God, the knowledge I've acquired is only an abbreviated form of the knowledge about natural science. But, it's been enough to bring new light to my mind and to get rid of the dark.

ANNE You said you've gotten rid of superstitious beliefs, does that mean you no longer believe in trolls and gnomes?

GUNDER That's what I said.

ANNE So you no longer believe in *hulder** or the little people?

---

*Among the spirits, trolls, and other creatures of Norwegian folklore are the forest-dwelling "hulder people." Human-like, the female "huldra" appears in numerous folktales as an attractive young woman and seductress. She possesses a troll-like tail that she tries to keep hidden, but which usually exposes her and causes her human prey to flee. The archetype of the huldra can be a young woman or a nagging wife who may have lost her tail as a result of marrying a Christian man, but has not lost the temper or threatening demeanor of the huldra.

GUNDER No, my dear, I've bid the *hulder* and the little people farewell. In the same proportion that enlightenment increases, the belief in such beings decreases. They cease to exist with the light of knowledge.

ANNE But, so many trustworthy people have assured us that they—

GUNDER *(interrupts)* Oh, Anne, all these trustworthy people aren't so trustworthy.

ANNE But, don't you remember what Kari Husevold told us what she saw one Midsummer?

GUNDER Oh, yes, I remember it very well.

ANNE Do you think that Kari Husevold is a woman who would tell something that isn't true?

GUNDER I think Kari Husevold is an honest and honorable woman who would never tell a lie. But many people, especially unenlightened people, who are stuffed full of stories about trolls from childhood, go around with the fear that they might see something strange and that sometimes makes them think that they actually did see something that enlightened people never see.

ANNE You must never say such things so that my father hears them.

GUNDER Why not?

ANNE He believes in things like that.

GUNDER That's exactly why I want to speak so he hears me. I want to use all my strength to work for the elimination of superstition and to spread enlightenment.

ANNE But father is impetuous and if you try to contradict his belief in magic and witchcraft, he'll get angry and chase you away, and then—

Scene 3: ANNE, GUNDER, PEER, ELSE

PEER and ELSE *(enter in haste)*

PEER I should have known! There you are! I suspected this would happen. Now do you see, Else, that something can easily happen to keep me from working?

ANNE What is it?

ELSE Hurry, Anne, find some linen, father has injured his hand.

PEER I should have known, it's as though something told me this would happen.

GUNDER Have you injured your hand?

PEER *(looks at Gunder)* Oh it's you, Gunder? Damn, I've crippled my hand. So you've returned now? Ow! Isn't she coming with the bandages? Welcome back, Gunder.

GUNDER Thank you, thank you.

PEER Ow! Damn!

GUNDER What happened?

PEER Oh, I was ready to use the sledge hammer, and—

ANNE *(enters with the linen rags)*

PEER Wrap it! Firmly!

ELSE No, the wound must be washed before it's wrapped. Anne, bring in some cold water.

PEER Cold water! Nonsense! Bring in the whiskey and saltshaker.

ELSE Are you crazy, Peer? You don't want to put whiskey and salt on it?

PEER Like I said, whiskey and salt. If you do as I ask, I would be most appreciative.

ELSE Yes, yes, as you will. Anna, bring in the whiskey and the salt, but bring in some cold water, too.

PEER *(sits down)* Uff! This hurts! *(to Gunder)* As I was saying, I was getting ready to use the sledgehammer and this dog jumped up on me, causing me to strike my hand, and— ow, ow! Are you crazy, Else, are you trying to burn me alive?

ELSE *(having first used whiskey and salt, she now rushes to wash with cold water)*

PEER Ah, that feels much better. It hurts like hell. That damn dog! It's not going to live much longer, mark my word. Now do you see, Else, accidents can happen sooner than you think? What did I say? Well,

well, Gunder, so you're back, are you? How long has it been, two years?

GUNDER Yes, exactly two years.

PEER I suppose you're an educated man now?

GUNDER Well, I'm not that educated, but I am a hundred times more enlightened than I was before.

PEER A *hundred* times? That's a lot in two years. You don't say. You become that much more enlightened? You can probably produce a hundred times more grain and potatoes than the rest of us too?

GUNDER No, you're wrong there. I haven't done agricultural study, I've been to the Folk High School.

PEER Yes, yes, I know where you've been. But they teach useful things at the Folk High School too, don't they?

GUNDER Yes, but not agriculture, except maybe some chemistry.

PEER Chemistry? What is that?

GUNDER Chemistry is the teaching about the original elements of things, the science about what makes up the original elements of everything.

PEER I don't understand that.

GUNDER For example, with the help of chemistry, we are able to say what is in this bottle and how much of various elements it contains.

PEER Well, I can tell you that without having gone to a Folk High School. It's made up of a half pint of alcohol and a half pint of salt. Ha, ha, ha, that wasn't difficult to know.

GUNDER Of course, you put it in the bottle yourself so you should know. But a chemist can tell us what elements make up the contents, even the blood in a person's body. He can tell me how much water, how much salt, and how much iron—

PEER *(interrupts with a surprised and skeptical look)* Iron? Iron? Iron, you say? Did you say there is iron in blood?

GUNDER Yes, there's iron in blood.

PEER Iron in blood? Ha, ha, ha, ha, no, now you're being funny. Iron in the blood—that's the best story I've heard in my whole life. It's too bad I didn't know that before because I occasionally bleed myself and I've always thrown the blood away. From now on, I'm going to take care of it, since it has iron in it. I buy lots of scrap iron, but I should be able to stop that now that I know that I only need to bleed myself a little. Ha, ha, ha, ha.

GUNDER I assure you, there is iron in blood.

PEER Ha, ha, ha, ha. Iron in blood! And you call yourself enlightened? Ha, ha, ha, ha. You educated people can sure come with a lot of stories to try to convince us simple folk. Ha, ha, ha, iron in blood?

GUNDER Yes, and there is also supposed to be silver and gold.

PEER Ha, ha, ha, no, this is getting better and better. Iron and silver and gold in blood. Why in the hell are they going to Australia to look for gold when they can find it in their own blood?

GUNDER I see that you find it all amusing, but it is not amusing. It would be better if simple people believed what enlightened people tell them about the contents of science than what all kinds of foolish and fraudulent people tell about spirits and trolls.

PEER Ha, ha, it looks like you have become so enlightened that you no longer believe in God or the Devil. Maybe you've become one of those who think that the world was created by itself?

GUNDER No, I don't believe that.

PEER Well, that's good. You still have some faith. But, let me tell you this, my dear Gunder, don't come here trying to spread your teachings of iron and silver in the blood. People will only laugh at you and call you a fool.

GUNDER Well, I'll just have to accept that. Fulton* faced the same fate when—

PEER Fulton? What kind of fool was that?

GUNDER He was a fool who claimed that man could sail a big ship against the wind without sails or oars, by just boiling some water in a

*Robert Fulton (1765–1815), an American engineer and inventor generally credited with developing the first successful commercial steam-powered ship in 1807.

kettle until it turned to steam. This fool is now marveled at and honored all over the civilized world, and there is no country that doesn't make use of his invention.

PEER *(angry)* But, wife, can't you see that the bandage is full of blood? I'm losing all my blood. Tighten the bandage! Anne! Pour out the water! No, dammit! Don't pour out the water, there's iron and silver in it. Ha, ha, ha, ha.

Scene 4: ANNE, GUNDER, PEER, ELSE, ERIK

ERIK *(enters)* Good evening.

PEER *(looks around)* Oh, is it you, Erik? Good evening! You've come just in time. I've hurt my hand by hitting it with a sledgehammer.

ERIK But, how in the world could that happen?

PEER Just as I was getting ready to strike, a dog jumped up on me and I hit my hand. I don't think it'll be too serious, but I won't be able to work for four or five weeks.

ERIK That's terrible.

PEER But something has just occurred to me. If I could only get in contact with Stub-Ingeborg, maybe I could be cured right away. You know that Stub-Ingeborg is very good at healing wounds. You remember that she cured Aslak Bolteløkka when he had gotten a troll in his knee?

ERIK Yes, and Ingeborg Bjønnerud was cured after no doctor was able to cure her.

GUNDER Did she try more than one doctor?

ERIK Tried? Well, she tried the doctor that we have, anyway. You know that too, Peer. In fact, Dr. Hansen checked on her for several weeks.

PEER He sure did! Oh, that Stub-Ingeborg is a strange woman. She's able to do things that no one else can. Erik, do you suppose she's home this time of day?

ERIK That's not so sure since she travels around from farm to farm healing both people and animals.

PEER Erik, couldn't you ask around where she might be and get in touch with her?

ERIK Y...e...s, I can probably do that, but I think she's at Lingonberry Moor over at Elling Braarud's house. I heard yesterday that one of his children was sick and that she was going over there. *(starts to leave)*

PEER No, wait a minute. If she's there, that's not so far. Anne can go. Anne! Go over to Elling Braarud and get Stub-Ingeborg to come over here—have her come back with you.

ANNE *(leaves)*

GUNDER Listen, Peer, I advise you to be careful with that hand and not let that gypsy woman tamper with it.

PEER Gypsy woman? Who are you calling a gypsy woman?

GUNDER That's what I call a woman who tries to swindle people.

PEER Has she swindled you, perhaps?

GUNDER No, and she won't, either.

PEER Then why do you call her a gypsy woman?

GUNDER Because she swindles people.

PEER She does *not* swindle people, I say!

GUNDER She claims to heal by magic signs and witchcraft; that makes her a swindler. Do you really think that she can cure your hand by saying a few words over it?

PEER I have to believe what I see with my own eyes, don't I?

GUNDER Sometimes we think we see something that isn't even there.

PEER Yes, that's true, and some people think they see iron in human blood. Ha, ha, ha.

ERIK Ha, ha, ha.

ELSE Yes, but, Gunder, it is true that Stub-Ingeborg cured Aslak Bolteløkka after he had gotten a troll in his knee.

GUNDER A troll in his knee! God help us, how can you believe that there are such things as a troll in a knee?

ELSE Why couldn't a troll get into your knee?

GUNDER Because there is no such thing as a troll.

PEER Ha, ha, ha, ha, well, now we finally have it.

ERIK There are too trolls, I've seen them.

PEER You know that Syvert Braaten was gone for three years. Didn't he tell us himself that he was kidnapped by trolls in the woods and put into the mountain where he was kept for three years?

GUNDER Ha, ha, ha, ha. And you believe stories like that?

PEER Of course I believe it. Syvert Braaten is not the kind of man who would have anything to do with magic.

ELSE *(to Gunder)* Haven't you heard about the stones thrown at the minister's mountain farm? Trolls threw giant stones through the window without breaking a single pane of glass. There was only one tiny little hole, no bigger than my hand, in the glass. Through that hole came all those giant rocks.

GUNDER But, how can you believe something so impossible?

PEER Impossible? But you're not the one who's impossible when you say there is iron and gold in human blood?

GUNDER But when it can be proven that—

PEER *(interrupts)* We've had enough of this nonsense and rubbish. No, these enlightened people don't believe in anything. I mean, it's true what I heard a minister say once, that all of this modern enlightenment is nothing but ungodliness.

GUNDER But you have to admit that if spirits and trolls existed, the enlightened people would see them just as much as the unenlightened ones.

PEER If the enlightened people only believed, they would see something, but it is their disbelief that causes them to see nothing.

GUNDER Yes, that's just what I mean. It's all just a matter of one's imagination.

PEER Imagination? You talk as though you have all the answers. You better watch out, young man, that the Evil One doesn't take you one day.

GUNDER Oh, if I don't do anything evil, I'm not afraid of the Evil One.

PEER Gee, how unusually wise people are these days. All it takes is for them to have read a little in some of these damned books of theirs and they think they've acquired all of the wisdom of the world. And now here comes this eighteen-year-old schoolboy laughing right in the faces of experienced folks. Shame on young people these days! Shame on the disbelieving times we live in! If I had the power, I'd chase all these unbelievers out of the country.

GUNDER But, fortunately, it is the forces of enlightenment that have the power in our times.

PEER Oh, don't come here spouting your enlightenment! I know more than ten little pups like you.

GUNDER I don't deny that you have ten times the experience, but—

PEER But, I don't know as much as you do?

GUNDER You may have more natural understanding, but—

PEER Will you now shut up, pretentious puppy that you are? Not one more word!

GUNDER Peer, don't get so worked up.

PEER Shut up, I said.

GUNDER But you can't deny—

PEER Will you shut up? Can't I even get peace in my own house? Get out! I don't want such smart people in my house.

GUNDER But, dear Peer.

PEER Get out, you Satan! *(takes hold of his collar and forces him out. Else tries to hold him back, but is pushed away)*

Scene 5: PEER, ERIK, ELSE

ERIK *(laughs maliciously)* Ha, ha, ha, ha. That was just what he deserved for his insolent behavior.

PEER At least I can keep my own house free from such people. Here comes this puppy pretending to be so much smarter than other folks and thinks he's such a wise man because he spent two years at this

Folk High School. If I had ten sons, I'd never send any of them to a devilish school like that.

ERIK I'm with you.

ELSE Peer, you shouldn't have treated Gunder like that. Gunder's a nice boy and you know he thinks a great deal of Anne.

PEER He'll not have Anne at any price, as sure as my name is Peer Olsen. Do you think I'd want a son-in-law who claims to be so smart and sees me as some kind of cruel and vulgar person? Well, no thanks! I'll sell my soul to the devil before he gets Anne.

ELSE Oh, heavens, don't talk like that, Peer. *(clasps her hands together)*

PEER Oh, yes, I'll talk that way if I want to.

ELSE But there is one thing you can't deny, that it's just us unenlightened people who still believe in trolls.

PEER Now, look here. You'd be better off to go down to the barn and look after the black cow; there's something wrong with her. Go down to the barn, I say!

ELSE *(shakes her head and goes)*

Scene 6: PEER, ERIK, ELSE, and ANNE *(outside)*, GUNDER *(in the window)*

ERIK *(looks carefully around)* Peer!

PEER What?

ERIK Can you keep a secret?

PEER Keep a secret? You know I can.

ERIK Do you remember we talked about the Black Book the other day?

PEER *(moves closer, looks around)* The Black Book, you say? Yes, if I could only get hold of that book, then I'd be saved.

ERIK I've got a copy of it. Shh!

PEER *(slowly)* The Black Book?

ERIK Yes, the Black Book, yes!

PEER The real Black Book?

ERIK Exactly, the real one—the ninth edition—that's the real one.

PEER Do you have it with you?

ERIK *(looks around)* Here it is. *(takes it out of his breast pocket)*

PEER Now, my fondest wish will be fulfilled. We have to lock the doors. *(locks them)*

ERIK But, this is a dangerous book, you know, nobody is able to burn it. There was once a farmer in Valdres who mocked the book and tried to show that it could burn just like any other book. He threw the book on a fire, but in that same instant, his house caught fire and burned down. When the house had burned, there in the ashes lay the Black Book, untouched.

PEER I know one must be careful with the Black Book. I know it's a dangerous book, but I've also heard that if one is careful and does exactly as is written in the book, and does not doubt, then one can do anything.

ERIK You've heard about—

ANNE *(knocks on the door)* Open the door!

PEER Stay out, you can't come in.

ANNE I was supposed to tell you that Stub-Ingeborg will come early tomorrow morning.

PEER Good! Now, go out to the barn with your mother, for the time being. Now, Erik, what were you going to say?

ERIK You've heard about the divining rod?

PEER Yes, it's a magic stick that shows where to find gold and silver.

ERIK Exactly! And if you make a divining rod in accordance with the Black Book, one can become very rich. You know, Mons Bokkelia became a rich man right away.

PEER Yes, people have always wondered where his money came from.

ELSE *(knocks)* Open the door!

PEER Stay out for a while! Stay in the barn! Continue, Erik!

ERIK Mons Bokkelia got his money with the help of the divining rod.

PEER Oh, I should have known that he got it in a strange way. Come on, Erik, let's make a divining rod.

ERIK Yes, you see, that's exactly why I came. I know you're a good blacksmith and that's the first thing. I know you can keep a secret, and that's important, and I know you have the belief. That is absolutely necessary.

PEER Come on, then, let's read.

ERIK Well, here you see it says: "The... divin...ing... rod... or... the... se... secret..." Oh, you read, you can read much better than me.

PEER *(reads)* "The divining rod or the secret art of finding hidden treasures of gold and silver."

ERIK Read more!

PEER "Does your soul thirst for gold and silver? Then I am the only one who can satisfy your thirsting soul." Who, "I"?

ERIK Oh, the "I" means the Evil One, of course. It's the Evil One himself who has written the Black Book.

PEER Oh, yes, of course, yes.

ERIK Continue.

PEER "Take a piece of hard steel and weld it together with copper made from three stolen copper coins to make a knife. Then go into the forest and cut a seven-year-old fir tree. Take the third branch of the tree and whittle a stick which is exactly thirteen inches long and one inch thick. Then read three times the divining rod verse found in this book but the verse must never be read aloud. Take the divining rod and hang it around your neck with a short ribbon. Wherever the divining rod points, you are to walk, and the divining rod will show you where to find gold and silver. All this is to be done on a Thursday night and you are to call my name."

(there is a long pause where both look at each other and all around)

ERIK Brr. I'm beginning to shiver.

PEER Don't you have any courage, Erik?

ERIK Yes, I have courage, but I'm so afraid. But, so what, I want some gold.

PEER That's right, Erik, we must have gold. That is, you will. *(offers his hand)*

ERIK *(shakes Peer's hand)* I will.

PEER You get the copper coins, I'll get the fir tree twig, and we'll meet here tonight. If all goes well, you'll be my son-in-law, Erik.

ERIK That's right, Peer. I'll be a good son-in-law. See you later. We'll meet tonight in the blacksmith shop. *(goes)*

PEER This is going to be fine. Ha, I'm going to get some gold. No more worries about the future. Now, I'll turn the proud heads of Huseby and Sonstevolden. *(makes a threatening gesture with his hands, goes out, leaving the door open)*

Scene 7: GUNDER, ANNE

GUNDER *(during the previous scene, he has been seen sticking his head in and out of the window. Now, he crawls into the room through the window)* Aha! So, it's the Devil's art that's being practiced here. The Black Book! Divining rods! Oh, yes, I know that history. With the help of the divining rod, we'll find silver and gold. What a pathetic superstition! What incredible ignorance!

ANNE *(enters on her tiptoes, listens, bumps into Gunder and lets out a scream)*

GUNDER What is it? Anne, is that you?

ANNE Is that you, Gunder?

GUNDER What are you screaming for?

ANNE Oh, God, you scared me. I thought it was the Evil One himself who got hold of me.

GUNDER The Evil One got hold of you? How could you come up with something like that?

ANNE Well, Gunder, something's not right in this house. *(whispers)* I think there's witchcraft being practiced.

GUNDER Oh, Anne, don't believe such things. Nobody can practice witchcraft.

ANNE *(slowly)* Father and Erik are dangerous together. I stood outside the door listening and I understood that they have a copy of the Black Book.

GUNDER So what?

ANNE Something dangerous is going to happen.

GUNDER What kind of book do you think this Black Book is?

ANNE It's a book that instructs on the art of witchcraft, isn't it?

GUNDER Who do you think wrote the Black Book?

ANNE It must be the Evil One himself who wrote and printed the book.

GUNDER No, my dear Anne. The Black Book was printed by a poor printer in Holmestrand. He probably got a teacher or a student prankster to put it together. You see, a poor printer has to find something to print that would sell and everyone knows that you can always make money by appealing to an ordinary person's superstitions.

ANNE Yes, it's quite possible that what you say is true, Gunder. But what is certain is that this must remain between the two of us.

GUNDER Just between us? Why? Don't you care for me anymore?

ANNE You know I do, Gunder. But no one can escape their fate, and it is my fate that I am to have someone other than you. Then it doesn't matter if I have my own will.

GUNDER Oh, one despairs over such superstition!

ANNE You call everything superstition, Gunder, but there is a greater power over us.

GUNDER Yes, indeed, my dear Anne, but the God who rules over us gave us reason and free will. We have reason so that we can use it to bring more and more light to our spirit, and free will so that we are not led blindly to an unhappy fate.

ANNE That may well be, Gunder. But what you are saying is above me. I think I'll stick with my simple belief.

GUNDER You're wrong, Anne. What I am telling you is simple. It is belief in witchcraft that is above us.

ANNE That may be as well, but it's clear that we can never have each other. Heaven help me, heaven help me; I think so highly of you, Gunder.

GUNDER You shall be mine, Anne, so Satan himself—

ANNE *(interrupts, covers his mouth)* Hush! Hush! Don't use the name of the Evil One. He is nearby. He is always near where the Black Book is.

GUNDER *(to himself)* The Black Book! *(stamps his foot)* The damn Black Book! *(to Anne)* If you will come with me, we will leave in secret. We'll flee to America and there we can get married in spite of all of this.

ANNE My God! What are you thinking about, Gunder?

GUNDER Your mother wouldn't have anything against it.

ANNE No, not mother, but father would. You don't know my father; if we do anything like that, he would kill us both.

GUNDER But once we're out on the Atlantic Ocean, he won't be able to get to us.

ANNE Well, then he'd send the Evil One after us. I truly think that he has made a pact with the Evil One.

GUNDER *(hits himself in the forehead in despair)* Oh, it's enough to drive a person mad. But, Anne, there are neither trolls nor spirits in America so, when we get there, we will be free from danger.

ANNE No, Gunder, you'll never get me to believe that.

GUNDER *(hits himself in the forehead)* No, this is too much, but it doesn't matter. If you must stay, ha, ha, ha, would I bow to superstition and stupidity and allow my bride to change me with witchcraft? No, my dear little troll! However much power you might have, I would show you my power too. *(ponders)* But, what shall I do? Assumptions don't work, arguing only makes things worse. I've got it! I'll use cunning against strength. I'll fight fire with fire. I'll get some gunpowder, some fuses, and rent a costume to dress up as the Devil. Then we'll see which devil is the strongest.

PEER *(outside – bangs the hammer)*

GUNDER Farewell for tonight, Anne. Dream about your Gunder, because he will be yours. *(rushes out through the window)*

ANNE *(goes to the window to see him go. After a pause, she begins to sing the opening song and, outside, Peer joins in, accompanied by the beat of the blacksmith's hammer)*

Change of scene: A forest.

Scene 8: PEER, ERIK, GUNDER

PEER and ERIK *(enter. Peer has the divining rod around his neck. Both walk quietly with careful steps. His arms moving erratically, Erik walks behind Peer, carrying two shovels)*

ERIK *(quietly)* Watch the divining rod if it doesn't turn now.

PEER I don't notice any change.

ERIK But it turned just the same.

PEER Yes, I think you're right. It turned to the left.

ERIK No, it was to the right.

BOTH *(take careful steps to the right)*

ERIK Now it's showing left.

PEER Well, let's turn then. *(they turn to the left)*

ERIK Hush! Hush! Did you hear something?

PEER No, I didn't hear anything. Did you hear something?

ERIK I thought I heard some rustling. Hush! *(they stand quietly, listening)*

PEER It's nothing. Hey, the rod isn't moving.

ERIK It's pointing nearby.

PEER Yes, it is.

ERIK It must be here, then.

PEER Yes, there must be gold and silver here.

ERIK Come on, let's dig. *(they begin to dig with the shovels)*

GUNDER *(in the woods, but not seen by Peer and Erik. After they have dug for a time, they hear a loud thunderclap and a flash of light with a strange whistling sound)*

ERIK *(sinks to his knees in fright)*

PEER Oh, that was only thunder.

ERIK Ooooh, did you hear that whistling?

PEER Oh, it's nothing, come on, we have work to do.

GUNDER *(thunders, lightning, and whistling sounds)*

ERIK *(throws away his shovel, sinks to his knees again)*

PEER You're a coward, that's what you are.

ERIK I— I'm going to die of fright.

PEER Get to work!

ERIK I don't dare anymore.

PEER Nobody's going to do anything to us.

ERIK But, what is that then?

PEER It's probably the trolls breaking the rocks in order to get at the gold for us.

ERIK D'you think so?

PEER What else would it be? Do you doubt the power of the Black Book?

ERIK Doubt? No, I don't doubt it. *(gets back on his feet)* Come on, let's get back to work.

PEER and ERIK *(begin digging again)*

PEER Stop, I found something. I found silver. *(picks it up)*

ERIK Gold, you say? *(grabs the stone)* Oh, it's just simple granite. We have to dig deeper. *(they dig deeper)*

PEER It's so hot here.

ERIK Hot? I'm freezing.

PEER You're just shaking, you coward!

GUNDER *(thunders violently, flashes of light. He points, screams; surrounded by fire, he comes forward in his devil costume. Melodrama:)*

ERIK *(throws himself flat on the ground)*

PEER *(throws the shovel and sinks to his knees)*

GUNDER *(grabs Peer's hand)*

PEER Oh, let me go! Let me go! Forgive me!

GUNDER You have called me although you have doubt and unbelief. You shall therefore be mine and go with me to my kingdom where fire will forever torture your eternal soul.

PEER I've done everything the book told me to do.

GUNDER But you have retained doubt in your heart.

PEER I have not doubted, it must be Erik who has doubted.

ERIK That's not true. I have not doubted, it is Peer who does not believe.

GUNDER *(to Peer)* Well, then you shall go with me to the Black Kingdom this instant. You will never again see your wife or your daughter.

PEER Mercy! Mercy!

GUNDER You will be devoured in my flames!

ERIK Huhuuu. I'll die of fright!

PEER Mercy! Mercy!

GUNDER No mercy! Come with me! *(because Gunder is occupied with Peer, Erik escapes by rolling away and out)*

PEER Mercy! Mercy! I promise to give you everything you demand.

GUNDER You promise everything I demand?

PEER Everything! Everything! Only please spare me!

GUNDER Can I trust you'll fulfill your promises?

PEER Test me!

GUNDER Well, I will test you, but remember this: if you break your promises, you will never be able to escape me.

PEER I will keep my promises.

GUNDER Very well, you must fulfill three promises and I will spare you!

PEER Yes, yes, yes!

GUNDER Give me the ring you have on your finger.

PEER *(gives the ring)*

GUNDER To the man who comes to you with this ring, you must give the hand of your daughter in marriage. Do you promise?

PEER I promise.

GUNDER You must give the Black Book to your son-in-law and ask him if he dares to doubt its power. Do you promise?

PEER I promise.

GUNDER But, what happened to your friend?

PEER He fled.

GUNDER Well, then you are to tell him that because he fled and thinks that he can escape my power, his punishment shall be that he brings bad fortune to any house where he stays longer than three minutes. Now, you can go, but remember well your promises.

PEER *(gets up carefully, feels his knees, stands and looks around nervously)*

GUNDER *(with slow, majestic steps, he steps back into the mountain with thunder and flashes of light)*

PEER *(when he no longer sees the Devil, he runs off)*

Scene 9: GUNDER

(during the monologue, Gunder gradually removes his Devil's costume)

GUNDER Ha, ha, ha. That's the way to frighten these superstitious people. I'm not surprised that in the old days Catholic priests used all kinds of tricks in order to control people. It is certainly tempting to use black magic in order to achieve one's highest dream which, for me, is to get Anne for a wife. I suppose I haven't won her in the most honest way, but when I become better acquainted with the old man, I'll make amends. And now, it's on to my dear Anne so that I can hold her in my arms. *(he exits)*

Change of scene: The original farmer's cottage.

Scene 10: ELSE, ANNE *(both enter)*

ANNE *(crying)*

ELSE You mustn't cry, Anne. If you continue like this you'll cry yourself to death in no time.

ANNE Well, I want to cry myself to death. I don't want to live anymore. What do I have to live for, life with a man who I can't stand. Oh, God, what an unhappy fate!

ELSE You don't want to live anymore? You want to die and leave me? Is that the way you show your love for me?

ANNE Oh, Mother, Mother, don't talk like that. I don't want to die and leave you, it's just that I'm so very unhappy.

ELSE Don't worry, my child. It's still possible that things can change for the better.

ANNE That will never happen, Mother. My fate is already decided.

ELSE Oh, things don't always go the way we think. Turn sincerely to Him who alone can comfort you in your unhappiness. *(exits)*

Scene 11: ANNE, GUNDER, ELSE

GUNDER *(enters, runs over to Anne and puts his arms around her)*

ANNE *(tries to get away)* No, no, Gunder! Get away from me. Why are you here again?

GUNDER I've come to see you.

ANNE Since we cannot have each other, that only makes things worse.

GUNDER But, now we can have each other.

ANNE That's only something *you* believe, Gunder.

GUNDER I don't *believe* it, I know it! Your father has given me his word.

ANNE *(suddenly happy)* What did you say? Father has given you his word? No, that can't be possible.

GUNDER You'll hear it from him yourself. Where is he?

ANNE I don't have any idea where he is. He and Erik stood for a long time at the blacksmith forge, then they went into the wood. Since then, I haven't seen them. I'm beginning to worry that the Evil One may have taken father.

ELSE *(enters)* What's happened to Peer? I'm worried that something bad has happened to him.

ANNE Yes, I'm worried about that too.

GUNDER Don't worry. He'll be home soon and in good shape, you'll see.

ELSE Hush! I hear footsteps!

ANNE He must be coming now.

Scene 12: ELSE, ANNE, GUNDER, PEER, ERIK

PEER *(enters, breathless, disoriented, does not see Gunder, throws himself on a chair with his face turned away from Else and Anne)*

ELSE What is it? What is it?

ANNE What is it, Father? Has something happened to you?

PEER Be quiet!

ELSE But, what is it then?

PEER What is it? That's *my* business.

ELSE You frighten me.

PEER Well, that's *your* business.

GUNDER Did something happen to you in the woods, Peer?

PEER *(hearing Gunder, he turns abruptly, gets up and makes a threatening gesture)* Are you here? What is this? You dare to come into my house, haven't I told you that—

GUNDER *(interrupts)* Oh, I'm sorry, but I was walking in the woods this evening and met someone who asked me to deliver this ring to Peer the Blacksmith, so— *(shows the ring)*

PEER *(takes the ring, pauses a moment, looks at the ring, looks at Gunder, remains silent, then suddenly takes Anne's hand and places it in Gunder's)*

ELSE *(clasps her hands together)* Is it possible?

ANNE Do you really mean it, Father?

PEER Shut up! *(squeezes their hands together)*

ELSE But, how could you have so suddenly changed your mind about Gunder?

PEER That's my business.

ANNE Thank you, Father, you have made me so happy.

GUNDER Thank you, Peer. *(offers his hand)*

PEER *(slaps Gunder's hand, then slaps himself on his forehead. He takes his copy of the Black Book from his breast pocket, extends it to Gunder, saying:)* Do you dare to doubt the power of this book?

GUNDER *(takes the book, looks at it)* Ha, ha, ha, this book has no more power than a wood chip.

PEER That's unfortunate! You better watch out for what you say.

GUNDER The best thing to do with this and other such books of witchcraft is to burn them all.

PEER Burn this book? *(derisively)* Burn this book? Burn this book, you say? No, my boy, you're too powerless for that.

ERIK *(stumbles in, goes over to Peer, takes his arm trying to lead him off to the side)*

PEER *(escapes Erik's grip)* Get out, you're bad luck!

ERIK What are you saying?

PEER Get out. Don't come into my house. What time is it? Gunder, let me borrow your watch!

GUNDER *(gives him his watch, whispers secretly to Anne)*

ERIK Have you lost your senses, Peer?

PEER Get out, I say, you've already been here one minute.

ERIK I mean it, you've lost your mind.

PEER For the third and last time, I'm telling you to get out. You're bad luck! You've been here for two minutes and if you aren't gone in thirty seconds, I'm going to kill you!

ERIK But, I have to talk with you, Peer.

PEER No talking, out! Out! *(picks up a chair and scares him into leaving)*

ANNE *(who had left the room when Gunder whispered to her, returns now holding a lit candle)*

GUNDER *(takes the candle and begins to burn the Black Book)*

PEER Are you crazy? If you do that, it'll mean the end of us all. *(holds his arm)*

GUNDER *(breaks loose and tries to light fire to the book)*

PEER *(blows out the candle, runs to the background, appears threatened)*

GUNDER *(in the meantime, he has lit a match that he has taken from his vest pocket and set fire to the book)*

ELSE and ANNE *(hold on to each other)*

PEER *(throws himself to his knees)* He's burning the Black Book! Now we're all doomed!

GUNDER *(as he's burning the book, he whistles a polka)*

PEER *(as he sees no immediate danger, he gets up, looks at the ashes of the book, then looks at Gunder, shakes his head, looks again at Gunder)* Tell me, *are* you Gunder Johannesen or are you a devil?

GUNDER Gunder Johannesen is my name.

PEER You, Gunder Johannesen has done something that no one else could ever do.

GUNDER What's that?

PEER Burn the Black Book!

GUNDER Any child of four could have done the same thing.

PEER *(puts his hands on Gunder, feeling if he is real)* Are you really Gunder Johannesen?

GUNDER Yes, of course that's who I am. What possible danger could there be to burn a worthless book such as that?

PEER *(clasps his hands together)* No, this is beyond anything I understand.

GUNDER So, Peer, you are allowing Anne to be my wife?

PEER Naturally!

GUNDER Will you keep your word?

PEER You can depend on it.

GUNDER Do you swear?

PEER I swear! *(raises his hand)*

GUNDER Well, my dear father-in-law, the first thing I want to do is to ask for your forgiveness.

PEER Forgiveness? For what?

GUNDER Because I have played a little comedy.

PEER Played a comedy? What do you mean by that?

GUNDER You see, I had to have Anne in order to be happy and Anne had to have me for her to be happy. Two people who love each other like that have a natural right to be together, but if they can't get together honestly, then sometimes deception must be used.

PEER I don't understand a word you're saying.

GUNDER Well, let me explain. That devil you met in the woods tonight and who forced you to make a few promises was none other than me, Gunder Johannesen.

PEER *(surprised, angry, and threatening)* Wh— wha— what? It— it was *you* who was the Evil One?

GUNDER Me and none other!

ELSE and ANNE *(surprised, they quietly look at each other)*

PEER Well, well, my dear Gunder. *(takes Anne and wants to pull her away from Gunder)* That puts a different light on the matter.

GUNDER Remember your oath!

PEER My oath? Yes, that's true! *(ponders)* That's true! I gave a sacred oath. *(ponders with his arms crossed)* Yes, yes, you know what, Gunder? When I think about it, everything seems to be in order, and you have burned the Black Book. That shows that either you were right when you said that the book was nonsense, or that you are stronger than the Evil One himself. In either instance, you deserve to be my son-in-law! But if this is the first comedy of this type that you have been responsible for, let it also be the last.

GUNDER *(to the audience)* Well, that depends on the audience.

CURTAIN FALLS

THE END